Distance Training

Despite the massive potential of distance learning on the World Wide Web, the field of distance training is little known or understood. *Distance Training: Taking stock at a time of change* provides a means to that understanding. It:

- presents research into four models of distance education, into which it is claimed nearly all provision worldwide falls;
- provides a global overview of distance education and training;
- examines case studies of distance education establishments providing insight into their structure and advantages;
- challenges the premise that distance training lacks academic excellence and status;
- appraises the role of distance education as a tool for employers to provide more effective and efficient training for employees.

Born in the nineteenth century, distance training came of age in the twentieth century. Desmond Keegan presents an overview of distance training from its inception and looks forward to the innovations of the future.

Desmond Keegan was foundation Chief Executive of the Italian Open University system and is currently Director of the Irish Centre for Distance Education Research and Applications.

RoutledgeFalmer studies in distance education
General Editors: Desmond Keegan and Alan Tait

Theoretical Principles of Distance Education
Edited by Desmond Keegan

Distance Education: New Perspectives
Edited by Keith Harry, Magnus John and Desmond Keegan

Collaboration in Distance Education
Edited by Louise Moran and Ian Mugridge

Otto Peters on Distance Education
Edited by Desmond Keegan

Theory and Practice in Distance Education
Börje Holmberg

Technology, Open Learning and Distance Education
A.W. (Tony) Bates

Open and Distance Learning Today
Edited by Fred Lockwood

Foundations of Distance Education, 3rd edition
Desmond Keegan

Opening Education
Edited by Terry Evans and Daryl Nation

Staff Development in Open and Flexible Learning
Edited by Colin Latchem and Fred Lockwood

Globalising Education: Trends and Applications
Robin Mason

The Convergence of Distance and Conventional Education
Edited by Alan Tait and Roger Mills

Open and Distance Learning in the Developing World
Hilary Perraton

Distance Training

Taking stock at a time of change

Desmond Keegan

London and New York

First published 2000
by RoutledgeFalmer
11 New Fetter Lane, London EC4P 4EE

Simultaneously published in the USA and Canada
by RoutledgeFalmer
29 West 35th Street, New York, NY 10001

RoutledgeFalmer is an imprint of the Taylor & Francis Group

© 2000 Desmond Keegan

Typeset in Times by
Keystroke, Jacaranda Lodge, Wolverhampton
Printed and bound in Great Britain by
MPG Books Ltd, Bodmin

British Library Cataloguing in Publication Data
A catalogue record for this book is available from the British Library

Library of Congress Cataloging in Publication Data
Keegan, Desmond.
    Distance training : taking stock at a time of change / Desmond Keegan.
        p.   cm. — (RoutledgeFalmer studies in distance education)
    Includes bibliographical references (p.) and index.
    ISBN 0–415–23065–9 (alk. paper) — ISBN 0–415–23066–7 (pbk. : alk. paper)
    1. Distance education.   2. World Wide Web.   I. Title.   II. Series.
    LC5800.K42 2000
    371.3′5—dc21   00-020130

ISBN 0–415–23065–9 (hbk)
ISBN 0–415–23066–7 (pbk)

Contents

Figures

Preface

'Distance education is the flavour of the month.' 'Get wired! Go digital! Build your web-based learning community!' 'Distance training is the harbinger of the new millennium.' 'Major corporations save millions of dollars each year using distance learning to train employees more effectively and more efficiently than with conventional methods.'

Such are the slogans of today.

A recent AltaVista search produced over 200,000 hits for the descriptor 'distance learning'.

In spite of this massive presence on the World Wide Web, and the claims that it has moved to the top of the educational agenda, the field of distance education and training is still little known and little understood.

Few understand the day-to-day workings of a university at which there are no students. Old and new stakeholders make conflicting claims about the field. Research viruses abound and there are few disinfectants. The interface between training on the World Wide Web and the open universities is little explored. There are few agreed rules for the choice of media, for quality control, for forecasting success or failure.

Purpose

The purpose of this book is to give an analysis and an overview of the whole sector of provision known as distance education and training.

For this purpose data are assembled from all over the world, especially Europe, the United States of America, and China, but from the rest of the world as well.

To concretise the data, sixteen institutional case studies are provided and sixteen national profiles.

Time of change

Born in the nineteenth century, distance training came of age in the twentieth century and is seen as a harbinger of the twenty-first century: a form of provision that had proved successful in the twentieth century and had characteristics that would be crucial in the next.

Subject to much criticism for its first 100 years, distance training grew in stature in the final three decades of the twentieth century, and achieved academic excellence at its close.

The electronics revolution of the 1980s greatly influenced distance training; the mobile and wireless revolution at the turn of the millennium again poses new challenges.

Cairncross's *The Death of Distance. How the Communications Revolution Will Change Our Lives* (1997) forecasts that distance will no longer determine costs of communication, location of communication, or size of message – all issues relevant to distance education.

The arrival of the net and the web into training in the late 1990s has seen the spawning of virtual universities. Will they wipe out conventional universities or distance universities or both or neither?

It is a time for taking stock. New stakeholders are entering the distance training industry market, and, like the new entrants into the telecommunications market, they are sleek and skilful with no history and little baggage.

From the Industrial Revolution through the Electronics Revolution to the wireless revolution

Distance training was impossible before the Industrial Revolution of the late eighteenth and early nineteenth centuries when for the first time it became possible to teach at a distance. Open universities and other individual-based distance teaching systems were born.

Group-based distance systems, and for the first time the possibility of teaching face-to-face at a distance, were born of the Electronics Revolution of the 1980s.

At the turn of the millennium the wireless revolution had already started with air interfaces replacing wired ones, and mobile phones and computers gaining ground over cabled and wired installations. Of little interest to campus universities, perhaps, but a new dimension and challenge for distance systems.

Distance education, distance learning, distance training

Distance education is used throughout in its legal sense of an institution contracting to provide internationally- and nationally-recognised university degrees, college diplomas and training certificates to students who are unable to, or choose not to, or refuse to, join other students at their centres for the purposes of learning. The term has other meanings but that is the focus here.

Distance learning is used throughout to describe group-based provision at a distance, where the use of the technologies of the Electronics Revolution enables groupings of students at a distance to be taught together by satellite or videoconferencing links. The term has other meanings but that is the emphasis here.

Distance training is used for the provision of professional and vocational qualifications at a distance. The term is interpreted broadly to include all vocational programmes at a distance at further education and at higher education level. The choice of the term *distance training* indicates that at least 70 per cent of distance programmes worldwide are at further education rather than at university level.

Foundations of Distance Education

It is 15 years since Croom Helm published *Foundations of Distance Education*, a repackaging of a PhD thesis which was designed to give a first overview of this field.

In 1990 the second edition was published, extensively rewritten to accommodate a paperback presentation, and the merger of Croom Helm and Routledge. It was reprinted a number of times and became a set text for many of the postgraduate diplomas or masters' degrees in distance education developed at that time.

One of the strengths of the first and second editions was an in-depth analysis of the socialist distance education systems of Central and Eastern Europe, which, with China, accounted for one-third of global provision in the 1980s. This had to be completely recast in the third edition, published in 1996, in the light of the political changes at the start of the 1990s and the abandonment of the socialist distance education model which followed.

It is pleasant to note that the still fragile and tentative status of distance education and training when *Foundations of Distance Education* was being drafted, has been replaced by the confident and vibrant state of the field today.

Distance Training. How Innovative Organisations Are Using Technology to Maximise Learning and Meet Business Objectives

Two American scholars (Schreiber and Berge) have recently published *Distance Training. How Innovative Organisations Are Using Technology to Maximise Learning and Meet Business Objectives*. This book provides a useful corollary to the present one, as it deals with in-house distance training in companies, non-profit-making organisations, and government agencies. The present book deals with distance training programmes that are available to the general public.

Themes

This book is about the sector of education and training provision dealing with those who do not attend training centres and colleges and universities. It hopes to contribute to the status and value of their studies and their awards.

This book is not about the use of technology in training centres, in colleges, in universities. It is about the use of technology for training those who do not attend them.

The book is not about promoting distance education and training. It is a book of analysis. It seeks to present the strengths and weaknesses of training at a distance.

The book addresses the tensions and the interfaces in the evolution from d-Learning to e-Learning to m-Learning. d-Learning is distance learning, e-Learning is electronic learning and m-Learning is mobile learning, based on the wireless technologies of the 21st century.

Acknowledgements

Some of the research on which this book is based was partially funded by different agencies and is gratefully acknowledged here.

In 1978, the Department of Further Education of South Australia contributed to an analysis of distance education worldwide. This enabled the fundamental structures of the field to be identified. In 1982, I had the honour to be invited as Visiting Professor of Distance Education to the ZIFF of the Fernuniversität in Hagen, where work was undertaken on the theoretical aspects of the field.

The World Bank sponsored a visit to China in 1989, during which the structures of distance education in China, and the development of work on mega-distance systems, especially in France and China, was started. In 1992, I was again invited to the Fernuniversität in Hagen as Visiting Professor and undertook further analysis of the theory and practice of distance education.

In 1994, a German Euroform project enabled a first census study of distance education in Europe to be undertaken. In 1995, an Irish Euroform project enabled research and analysis of distance education by satellite to be undertaken at University College Dublin, and the development of two-way videoconferencing training. In 1996, a grant from Directorate General XXII in Brussels enabled a further census study of the field in Europe to be undertaken. In 1997, a Leonardo Da Vinci project from the European Commission in Brussels contributed to a further census of distance training in Europe. In 1998 and 1999, Leonardo Da Vinci projects on courses on the internet contributed to work on distance training and the World Wide Web.

But most of one's major insights on a subject like distance education and training come from discussions with friends. Among the colleagues and friends I would like to thank are the following, many of whom have agreed to become members of the Advisory Board of the Irish Centre for Distance Education Research and Applications (ICDERA): Cheryl Amundsen of Vancouver, Manfred Delling of Tübingen, Xingfu Ding of Beijing, Helmut Fritsch of Frönsberg, Keith Harry of Milton Keynes, Ted Leath of Derry, Rory McGreal of Fredericton, Maggie McVay of Columbus, Emma Nardi of Rome, Morten Flate Paulsen of Oslo, Otto Peters of Hagen, Torstein Rekkedal of Bekkestua, Raymond Steele of Muncie, Benedetto Vertecchi of Frascati and Wei Renfang of Nanjing.

My secretary, Pamela Turley, did an excellent job of preparing the text for Routledge.

My wife and family are the inspiration for all I do.

WebCT™ Courses, Campus, Community gave permission for the use of Figure 10.2 and permissions to use other illustrations were given by Greville Rumble of *Open Learning*, Rory McGreal of TeleEducation, New Brunswick, Morten Flate Paulsen of NKI and Ted Leath of Magee College. These permissions are gratefully acknowledged.

Desmond Keegan
Dublin

1   Global overview at a time of change

Introduction

Distance training has come of age. In the 15 years since the publication of *Foundations of Distance Education* it has moved centre stage in the provision of education and training. Distance learning is an issue today for all training centres, business corporations and universities.

The end of a century which distance education and training entered as a highly criticised fringe form of provision, and ended as a harbinger of the new millennium, is an appropriate time for taking stock. The impact on distance systems of electronic technologies from the telecommunications and information communications industries, joined by the arrival of the internet and the World Wide Web, is a milestone from which there is no turning back.

The distance training industry market is sizeable and hotly contested by new and old providers.

The aim of this book is to provide the reader with an overview of this whole sector of educational and training provision in a concrete and factual way, so that the progress of recent decades can be charted, and the way to the future planned from correct foundations.

To evaluate adequately a whole sector of educational provision one needs to collect data globally.

Particular attention is paid in this book to presenting findings from research in the United States of America, in China, and in Europe, but provision in the rest of the world – Australia, the rest of the Americas, Africa, and the rest of Asia – is not neglected, and influences the analyses presented.

The goal is to show the richness and complexity of this form of training provision.

The two modes of distance education and training

When the global data are analysed they are clustered around two poles, here called the two modes of distance education and training: group-based distance training and individual-based distance training.

When one is planning a training system, whether face-to-face or at a distance, it is of crucial importance – both didactically and administratively – to establish if one is dealing with a learning group or with an individual.

In the literature, *distance learning* is usually used for group-based distance provision, whereas individual-based systems are here called *distance training*.

The group-based systems of today are largely based on rapid advances in communications technologies associated with what may be called the Electronics Revolution of the 1980s, which made it possible for the first time in history to teach face-to-face at a distance.

The individual-based systems of today use technologies from both the Electronics and the Industrial Revolutions, which made it possible for the first time in history to teach at a distance. Training on the web, although it can be used for synchronous events, is largely an asynchronous medium, and sitting in front of one's computer screen for the whole length of the training process is essentially an individual mode of training.

Group-based distance training

As the third millennium starts, the impact of distance systems is demonstrated by the development of both group-based distance training systems, and systems for individual learners.

In this analysis, group-based systems are divided into systems for full-time students and systems for part-time students, whereas systems for individual learners are best described as those that provide pre-prepared learning materials, or those that do not provide pre-prepared materials.

Group-based distance training links the teacher and the learners in several geographic locations by simultaneous audio, video, or satellite links, to a network of remote classrooms.

Group-based distance training for full-time students

Research on the Chinese *Zhongguo guangbo dianshi daxue (Dianda)* system in 1989 (Keegan 1993) showed that it was a network of radio and television universities for largely group-based, full-time students. The *Dianda* network uses satellite technologies to reach groups of students throughout the country.

Television and other distance learning materials are produced, mainly, by the Central Chinese Radio and Television University (CRTVU) in Beijing, which prepares the materials but does not enrol students. The television lectures are distributed by satellite links to students enrolled in, and grouped at, the 44 open universities throughout the country, where tutors are present and learning materials are studied.

The statistics show that 97 per cent of those enrolled in the *Dianda* network in the mid-1980s were full-time students at a distance, with the figure dropping to 16 per cent recently. Total enrolment varied between 500,000 and 800,000 per year.

Today the percentage of full-time students is below 10 per cent as the spread of the capitalist ideology in China has largely eliminated study leave for distance training.

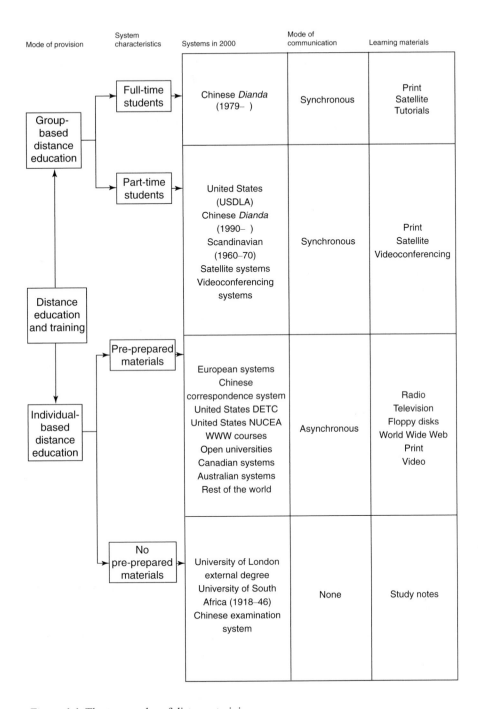

Mode of provision	System characteristics	Systems in 2000	Mode of communication	Learning materials
Group-based distance education	Full-time students	Chinese *Dianda* (1979–)	Synchronous	Print Satellite Tutorials
	Part-time students	United States (USDLA) Chinese *Dianda* (1990–) Scandinavian (1960–70) Satellite systems Videoconferencing systems	Synchronous	Print Satellite Videoconferencing
Individual-based distance education	Pre-prepared materials	European systems Chinese correspondence system United States DETC United States NUCEA WWW courses Open universities Canadian systems Australian systems Rest of the world	Asynchronous	Radio Television Floppy disks World Wide Web Print Video
	No pre-prepared materials	University of London external degree University of South Africa (1918–46) Chinese examination system	None	Study notes

Distance education and training

Figure 1.1 The two modes of distance training

In the 1980s the full-time students in the *Dianda* system received three years' study leave on full pay to complete their degree. They travelled on a daily basis to their factory or workplace, where they went to the education centre, rather than to their place of work. Their daily study programme began with the first of the live television lectures from Beijing, and these lectures were interspersed with tutor-led discussions and assignment work.

In the category of group-based distance education for full-time students one should also include much of children's distance study.

Distance education for children was initiated by the Australian state governments from 1914. By the mid-1920s all the state and provincial governments of Australia, Canada and New Zealand had a full-time distance education provision for children. Added to these later were the Schools of the Air for outback children in Queensland, New South Wales and South Australia where short-wave radio links and, today, web-based links, unite isolated students on large farming properties in class groupings.

More recently, since 1939, the French government, through its Centre National d'Enseignement à Distance (CNED), has provided a full-time distance education provision for children globally.

The scientific importance of studying group-based distance training for full-time students is that it gives important data and can correct research viruses in studies which have been undertaken without counting the full-time students.

Full-time distance students, for instance, do not drop out any more than students in full-time face-to-face provision. They take the same length of time to study a diploma or degree programme as students in conventional colleges or universities. Children also do not drop out from distance education programmes, nor do they take longer for their studies than their counterparts in schools.

Group-based distance training for part-time students

Just as the technological developments of the Industrial Revolution in the mid-nineteenth century brought students worldwide the benefits of individual-based distance education, so the technological developments of the Electronics Revolution in the 1980s brought students the benefits of group-based distance education.

This is the dominant mode of provision today in the US, where distance learning has become a major form of educational provision and of business training. It has an active organisation, the United States Distance Learning Association (USDLA), to promote its interests. This professional distance education association groups multinational and corporate providers with the universities. This mode of distance education comprises pre-prepared materials, satellite lectures and individual study at home.

In practice, distance learning can mean that the university professor, at a large number of US universities, proceeds to the lecture theatre to deliver his or her lecture to the students assembled there, and the lecture is up-linked to a satellite, from which it is down-linked to groups of students assembled in other locations throughout the state or the nation. These students are usually linked to the central lecture theatre by a telephone hook-up.

One-way video, two-way audio satellite, or two-way video, two-way audio compressed videoconferencing, are perhaps the dominant technologies at the start of the third millennium, but a wide range of options is available.

At the turn of the millennium, most of the hundreds of thousands of students in the Chinese *Dianda* system are properly located in this category, as part-time training has replaced full-time study at a distance.

European theorists have been slow to acknowledge the rapid spread of group-based systems as a complement to the individualised systems with which they are more familiar. The dimensions of the field cannot be appreciated without considering both modes. Misunderstandings in the literature can arise from trying to treat both modes of provision identically, without appreciating the crucial didactic and logistical differences between teaching adults in groups or as individuals.

Similarly, another standard form of provision of group-based distance training in the US, two-way video, two-way audio compressed digital videoconferencing, has also had little success in Europe.

In the US, it is regarded as a suitable form of provision for, say, a masters degree in nursing at the University of Albuquerque, in which full-time nurses, working in hospitals as much as 300 kilometres from Albuquerque, take their courses. In American practice, it is considered sensible to provide these professional qualifications, even at a videoconferencing rate as low as 112k (kilobytes) per second, to students who would otherwise have to drive 300 kilometres to Albuquerque, after a long day's work in the hospital, and then drive the 300 kilometres back, to resume work in their hospital.

Individual-based distance training

Over the last 150 years nearly all European distance training has been individual-based with pre-prepared materials. This has tended to focus European practitioners and theorists on this mode of provision. Again it is possible to identify two subsystems: systems based on pre-prepared materials and systems without pre-prepared materials.

Individual-based distance education with pre-prepared materials

Developments of communication technologies in the 1840s in Northern Europe and North America, laid the basis for training at a distance. For the first time it became possible to separate the teacher from the learner, and the learner from the learning group, and for students to learn from teachers individually at any place or at any time they chose.

Individual-based distance systems are to be found worldwide. The major characteristics of these systems are the scientific preparation of distance materials for individual learners, and the design of student support systems for students studying individually at a distance.

In this way, students worldwide benefit from being freed from the tyranny of timetabling: travelling at fixed times and on fixed days to join other persons at universities and training centres for the purpose of being trained. Learning systems were also freed from streaming: the inherent characteristic of conventional face-to-face, group-based education and training in which students of varying intelligence and of varying study backgrounds, and of varying degrees of motivation, are taught the same content in the same groups. The invariable result has been that the highly intelligent and the highly motivated students have been held back, with the slower or inferior learners also learning less than they might.

The rapid development of the internet in the years from 1995 has created a new global dimension for this form of training provision, as individuals all over the world study for degrees or other qualifications from their computer screens either at home or at work.

As the third millennium commenced, the wireless linking of students travelling at a distance in individual-based distance systems, with pre-prepared materials, is the latest possibility, creating not just students studying at a distance, but the student studying while travelling at a distance as well.

Most of the European systems are correctly located in this classification whichever of the four major models developed in this book they follow: the open university model, the government distance training institution model, the private distance training institution model, or the provision of training at a distance from conventional universities model.

In spite of the extensive provision of group-based distance education in China, there is very extensive provision of individual-based distance education as well.

At least one million students in China are enrolled each year in programmes which can be labelled correspondence education. There are several kinds of correspondence education in China but by far the largest is that sponsored by the conventional universities. It is widely used in teacher training and general higher education, as, for example, at the People's University in Beijing. Correspondence education has been localised by the various Chinese universities in their surrounding areas but has nationally become the biggest contributor of diploma and degree graduates at a distance to higher education.

In spite of the extensive provision of group-based distance education from conventional universities in the US, there is a large provision of individual-based distance education with pre-prepared materials as well.

In the proprietary sector, these providers are grouped in the Distance Education and Training Council (DETC), based in Washington DC, which comprises military, church and business organisations providing training at a distance throughout the US.

Allied to this is the provision through universities affiliated to the the National University Continuing Education Association (NUCEA), which comprises departments in many US universities, which provide distance training courses to individual students studying at a distance, rather than the electronic groupings of students analysed in the previous section.

There is now little doubt that the World Wide Web is the most successful educational and training tool to have appeared in a long time. It can be used on a global scale and is platform independent. In spite of the possibility of linking distance students electronically and synchronously on the WWW, the vast bulk of web-based provision is properly located in the category of individual-based distance education with pre-prepared materials.

Individual-based distance education with pre-prepared materials is the proper location for nearly all the open universities throughout the world. Many of the open universities were founded in the 1970s and 1980s and are now national institutions of great prestige and excellent quality. Few are new or experimental. Most have decades of experience and tens of thousands of graduates already integrated into the national workforce. Such institutions form an important focus for the study of distance training and underline the contribution that this form of provision makes in developed and emerging economies alike.

Most Canadian and Australian systems would also correctly be located in the category of individual-based distance training with pre-prepared materials. Systems in the rest of the world, which do not clearly fall into the group-based distance training categories in the classification provided, are also located here.

Individual-based distance training without pre-prepared materials

The external degree programme of the University of London dates from about 1840 and is ongoing today. This individual-based distance provision without pre-prepared materials predates the development of pre-prepared materials for distance systems, usually estimated to have started in the years 1855 to 1880.

Simply put, these systems enrol individual students at a distance and, in the case of the University of London, from all over the world, and provide the enrolled students with syllabuses, content description, reading lists and previous examination papers.

The students then choose their method of study. They can study at a local college or a university – if they can find a programme that resembles the distance programme in which they are enrolled. Many of the British distance education colleges, like Wolsely Hall, started precisely to provide courses for the University of London external degree programme. Alternatively the students can study completely individually, buy or borrow the textbooks on the reading list, and then present themselves for the examination.

The University of South Africa ran a similar system from 1910 to 1946, at which date it commenced the design and production of pre-prepared distance education materials.

There is a thriving system in China today, with about one million students enrolled each year. This system is often referred to as the self-taught higher education examination system. The system was established in the 1980s and is today carefully regulated by the Chinese Ministry for Higher Education.

The participants in this programme are better termed examinees than students. The system during the 1980s and 1990s has developed as an independent distance learning system, and as a regulatory system for adult education in general, and as a system linked to the other two large systems in China, the *Dianda* system and correspondence education.

Conclusion

In the twenty-first century, as in the century just ended, the task of distance training, research and management, will be the analysis of, and the provision of, courses for the students who wish to get a university degree or a training qualification, but who are unable to, or who choose not to, or who reside too far from, or who are blocked by other reasons from being able to reside at or travel to universities or training centres.

This chapter gives a framework for analysis to show how the group-based provision of the new electronics developments of the 1980s, the web-based initiatives of the 1990s, and the mobile communications of the 2000s, can be accommodated within a global classification that gives the reader an immediate overview of a whole sector of training provision.

The two modes of distance training are an important framework for analysing and for making management decisions on training and on degree programmes in virtual and distance training. The different dimensions of group-based and individual-based systems demonstrate the extent and importance of the field. Confusion can arise where the reader's attention is not drawn to the essential didactic and logistic differences, between training students as individuals or training them in groups.

2   From the Industrial Revolution to the Electronics Revolution

Tensions

This chapter highlights tensions in the field of distance training. There are tensions between group-based systems and individual-based systems. There are tensions between the technologies of the Industrial Revolution and the technologies of the Electronics Revolution. There are tensions between those who promote the WWW as the killer-application for distance training, and those who see value in other technologies for learning at a distance. There are tensions between wired, cabled and fixed technologies, and mobile technologies.

Above all there are tensions between those who see technological innovation in universities and training centres as the way forward, and those who focus on the training of the largely home-based learner at distance.

The Industrial Revolution

Distance education and training were born of the developments in technologies associated with the Industrial Revolution in Northern Europe and North America in the late eighteenth and early nineteenth centuries.

It was no accident that teaching at a distance began with the development of industrial technologies, especially in postal communications and transport. The first trains and the first correspondence courses started at the same time.

Even today distance training would not be possible in a society that had not yet achieved an adequate level of industrialisation.

It is of interest that the government of North-Rhine Westphalia chose to locate its open university at Hagen, because the wire- and needle-making industries in the valleys of the Hönne, the Ihmertebach, the Oese and the Lenne, at towns around Hagen like Hemer, Iserlohn and Altena, were the harbingers of the Industrial Revolution from the 1680s onwards.

It is an interesting coincidence that the theory of distance training as the most industrialised form of teaching and learning was developed by Peters (1994) who was to become the first *Rektor* of the Distance University at Hagen.

The Electronics Revolution

The telecommunications industry underwent swift and complex changes in the 1980s, which constituted an Electronics Revolution. These changes can be attributed to three factors:

- an urge to deregulate
- speeding up of chips
- introduction of broadband technologies.

Prior to the Electronics Revolution, governments regarded telecommunications as a lucrative, monopoly industry. It was linked to secret defence installations. There was total regulation. Development contracts were negotiated between the few monopoly providers and the military or government contractors.

Policies, however, associated with the Thatcher government in the UK led to open tenders, and a quest for improved services, and better value for government money.

Policies associated with the Reagan government in the US led to the breaking of monopolies, especially for the new cellular licences. Telecommunications became consumer-driven.

Computing technology was introduced into telecommunications in the 1960s with the first public, analogue software switchboards dating from the mid-1970s. These were digitalised almost immediately, and were followed by the development of Integrated Services Digitalised Networking (ISDN) in the 1980s. In the 1990s, seamless digitalised connections between fixed and air networks were achieved. In all these developments, the ever-increasing speed of chips was crucial. The process will be accelerated with the replacement of silicon chips by nano-chips in the early 2000s.

The development of broadband technology is of vital importance for distance training, because one needs extensive bandwidth for pictures, audio, video and virtual realities. Broadband is usually defined as rates of more than two mb (megabytes) per second over a public switched network. Interactive multimedia, image processing, data and video are all large consumers of bandwidth.

The Electronics Revolution of the 1980s led to group-based distance training and opened the way to the net and the web.

A Mobile Revolution

In late 1999 the population of the world reached six billion for the first time. Almost the same day Ericsson and Nokia announced that there were 500,000,000 mobile phones in the world and there would be one billion by 2004.

The Mobile Revolution has arrived.

The Electronics Revolution of the 1980s changed the nature of distance education, making it possible to teach face-to-face at a distance, to restore eye-to-eye contact electronically, and to teach groups as well as individuals at a distance. The Mobile Revolution of the late 1990s will change the distance student from a citizen who chooses not to go to college, to a person who not only chooses not to go to college, but is moving at a distance from the college.

The development of the didactic structures for the implementation of the Mobile Revolution will fall largely to the open universities and the government distance-training systems, as there is little likelihood that universities will focus didactically on students who choose to be mobile away from them.

If there is a rule about the choice of technology for distance training it is that technologies that are available to citizens may succeed. Rarely has a technology penetrated society so quickly and so widely as the mobile telephone.

There is an unprecedented takeup of wireless telephones and wireless computers in developed and developing countries alike. The World Wide Web and the internet are not enough, says the telecommunications industry: wireless access independent of location and internet services everywhere are the requirement. The air interface is replacing the wire interface.

At the time of writing we have only seen the beginning of the wireless information society. But the protocols for provision are already being put in place: Bluetooth, GPRS, WAP.

Bluetooth is the universal radio interface for wireless connectivity. Previous portable devices used infrared links, were limited to two metres, were sensitive to direction, needed direct line-of-sight, could only link two devices. By contrast, the Bluetooth air connectivity uses radio links, which have much greater range, can function around objects, can go through certain materials, can connect to many devices at the same time.

General packet radio system (GPRS) brings official data and internet connectivity to mobile terminals giving instant, transparent, IP (Internet Protocol) access with no call set-up time. Wireless access protocol (WAP) brings web browser usability of the Internet to mobile terminals. It provides data-oriented, non-voice services, anywhere and at any time. The major manufacturers are committed to global standardisation of third generation mobile systems in radio environments like wide-band code division multiple access.

The challenge for distance systems at the dawn of the third millennium is to develop didactic environments for mobile phones and mobile computers as the availability of mobile devices spreads to a billion users. The mobile telephone is becoming a trusted, personal device with Internet access, smart card usage, and a range of possibilities for keeping the distance student in touch with the institution's student support services, in contact with learning materials and fellow students, while at home, or at work, or travelling.

Teaching

The Industrial Revolution and the Electronics Revolution had major impacts on education and training.

Historians of education in the East (Wei 1997) and in the West (Boyd and King 1969) trace back the origins of organised teaching for more than 2000 years.

Boyd and King, and most modern textbooks on the history of western education, start in Ancient Greece with Socrates and Plato 2,350 years ago. The features of this form of education, the dialogue, the dialectic, and the analysis, have been characteristics of western education ever since.

The medieval universities added the lecture, the humanists the seminar and the tutorial. Today the characteristics of education in schools, colleges and universities are: face-to-face education, between teacher and learner in the learning group, based on interpersonal communication.

In the East the development of higher education is traced back to Confucius and beyond. The Confucian idea of education came from belief in the natural goodness of man. This idea became established in feudal society and individual achievements and personal advancement were subordinated to the good of society. Education, therefore, was based on the learning group and provided to groupings of students.

Teaching at a distance

The history of distance teaching began less than 150 years ago. The developments of technology associated with the Industrial Revolution in Northern Europe and North America made it possible for the first time in history to teach at a distance.

What is essential to distance education is the separation of teacher from learner, and of the learner from the learning group. Distance education recognised that teaching and learning are separate acts that can safely and effectively be carried out by means of communications technology, even though teacher and learner are separated in space and time.

Distance education is characterised by the replacement of interpersonal face-to-face communication in the learning group, by an apersonal mode of communication mediated by technology. As a result, the first 100 years of distance education were characterised by doubts and criticism. But the development of open universities throughout the world in the 1970s brought rapid improvements in the quality, the quantity and the status of provision.

Teaching face-to-face at a distance

The telecommunications technologies associated with the Electronics Revolution of the 1980s made it possible to teach face-to-face at a distance.

Virtual or electronic classrooms are linked in this development by compressed video codec (coder/decoder) technology along telephone lines enabling a class of students to be divided between two cities or two countries.

The lecturer can see and hear, not only the students present at the class, but all the other students at the other sites hundreds or thousands of kilometres away. In the same way, all the students at all the locations can see and hear not only the lecturer but all other students in the system. All the interaction of face-to-face education has been recreated electronically: any student can question or interrupt the teacher or another student, just like in a normal classroom. It is now electronically possible to teach face-to-face at a distance.

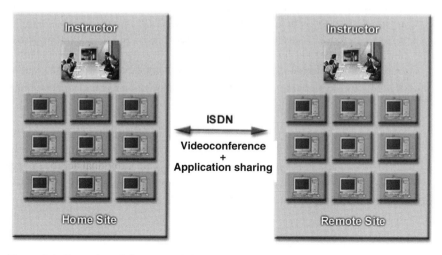

Figure 2.1 Group-based distance training by videoconferencing

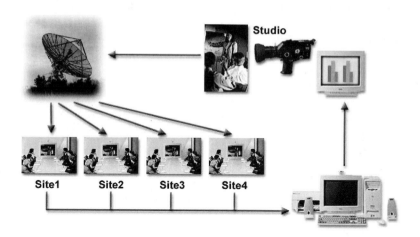

Figure 2.2 Group-based distance training by satellite

Distance teaching had brought great benefits to those citizens who could not, or chose not to, attend the schools, colleges or universities of the world but it lacked interpersonal interaction and, above all, the eye-to-eye contact of conventional education.

As the eye is the organ of a person's innermost feeling, argues Peters, this absence of eye-to-eye contact is surely significant. 'We become aware that a whole emotional dimension of the interaction of the teacher and learner is lacking in distance education' (1994:214).

As the twenty-first century arrives, the provision of education to citizens around the world is enriched by the availability of conventional face-to-face teaching in schools, colleges and universities, complemented by correspondence, audio, video and computer technologies from correspondence schools and open universities throughout the world. Both are enriched by the availability of virtual systems in which the face-to-face interpersonal communication of conventional education can be achieved at a distance.

Complex processes by which people learn

Underlying any analysis of the choice of technologies for distance learning is research on unravelling the complex processes by which people learn. Cognitive theories of learning offer more comprehensive, though still incomplete, explanations of the neural processes in which learning occurs, than did the behaviourist positions which have been dominant in distance training in the past. Failure to apply these positions to the design of distance training course development procedures and student support services, both in electronic and non-electronic systems, should lead to lack of success.

McVey (1970) of the University of Wisconsin, Madison, and others in the 1960s, had worked out the laws for learning from screens. Laws for audience volume, the minimum, optimum, and maximum viewing distance, the ratio of the width of a screen filling the visual field when located two screen widths from the viewer. In the early to mid-1990s the distance training by videoconferencing industry appeared to be unaware of this body of research.

Winn (1990) in a series of important research studies reported on many aspects of instructional/educational technology. His findings on the control of cognitive process by means of carefully selected instructional strategies, including visual cognitive process, the assessment of new information, and learning by means of analogy, are all relevant to training on the web.

Many years of research on learning with media are presented by Kozma (1991) who views learning as an active, constructive process whereby the learner strategically manages the available cognitive resources to create new knowledge, by extracting information from the environment and integrating it with information already stored in memory.

He gives the rules for learning with books, learning with television, learning with computers, learning with multimedia, and his work could easily be extended to learning on the web. The stability of text in constructing meaning, its referability, suitability for revision, and for summaries, overviews, rereading, moving back and forth in the text, and between texts, are emphasised.

Distance training is linked essentially to technology and evolves as new generations of technologies appear.

Major issues at the dawn of the third millennium include: What are the correct technologies for distance education and training? What are the didactic technologies of conventional education and training? Can the technologies of conventional and distance education be said to be converging? Why have there been so many mistakes in the choice of technologies for distance learning? Will the World Wide Web prove to be the decisive breakthrough for distance learning? What will be the impact of wireless technologies?

The chapter concludes with an application of these issues to a practical case – the foundation of the Open University of the United States – and with a look at the future.

Distance training technologies today

What is the choice of technology today for distance students who do not go to university or to a training centre?

The technologies of distance education are well known. The OUUK, for example, lists the technologies it sends out to its students as shown in Figure 2.3.

1,100,000	Audio cassettes per year
340,000	Floppy disks per year
130,000	CD-Roms per year
50,000	Students on line at home
70,000,000	E-mails sent per year
700,000,000	E-mails read by students per year

Figure 2.3 Technologies of the OUUK 1999

These uses of technology are in addition to the well-known printed learning materials, television programmes, and home experimental kits. The astonishing interchange of e-mails, presumably academic and social discussions, constitutes a new university discussion forum, as yet little known to academics elsewhere.

A 1999 investigation at a leading European university on the technology of conventional education identified three leading didactic uses:

- The overhead projector
- The whiteboard
- Periods of research on the university's computers.

The overhead projector was rated at over 100 per cent in the study, meaning that it was switched on before the students entered the lecture room, and was not switched off until after they had left.

This contrast between the technologies of the conventional university and the needs of distance students is clear. The didactic value of the overhead projector is only for students who travel to the university on the day in question; from this, distance students are by definition excluded.

Similarly the white board is a technology that excludes the distance students as its didactic use necessitates the student to join the learning group at fixed times on fixed days, a rhythm unsuitable for fully-employed taxpayers studying for a degree.

This book takes it as axiomatic that universities are centres of high technology and that corporate and government-training centres are often highly equipped with advanced-level technologies. Many universities are wooed by multinational corporations because of their expertise in technology. Many have high-powered web-linked computers – but the distance students choose not to use them.

Choice of technologies for distance training

Considerable controversy has characterised the choice of media for distance training. The choices made by the OUUK, detailed in Figure 2.3, show a careful selection from the available technologies.

Many other systems have been swayed by the technology in vogue at a particular time. Programmed learning machines were introduced with much the same research viruses that have characterised the introduction of most new technologies to distance education since:

*   deficiencies in research design
*   small samples
*   short trials
*   inadequate statistical treatment
*   evangelism
*   inconclusive results
*   aggressive messianism
*   no repetition of research.

This can be demonstrated by checking backwards through the journals of instructional and educational technology for articles on the ultimate choice of technology for distance training.

A pattern similar to that in Figure 2.4 emerges (see p. 17).

In spite of this history of the difficulty of arriving at final solutions, Collis claims that 'The WWW is the "killer AP" for telelearning.'

> It is now clear that the World Wide Web is the most potent technology to have become available to the distance training industry for many a day. Will it prove the 'killer application' for which many have been waiting? The distance training industry needs guidelines to make informed judgements on questions like these. (1996:531)

This analysis of the importance of the World Wide Web in training systems today is taken up in Chapters 9 and 10.

1930s	Programmed learning machines
1940s	Educational radio
1950s	I6mm film
1960s	Educational multimedia and audiovisual approaches
1970s	Instructional/educational television
1980s	Computer-mediated communication/CBL (computer-based learning)/ CML (computer-managed learning)/CBT (computer-based training)
1990	Prestel
1991	12" laser disks
1992	Audiocassettes and video recorders
1993	Interactive video
1994	Videoconferencing
1995	CD-Roms
1996	The Internet
1997	The WWW
1998	Java applets in web-based courses
1999	Streaming audio and video

Figure 2.4 Choices of media for distance training

United States Open University

In 1999 the OUUK announced the formation of the United States Open University at Wilmington, Delaware, and that it was a candidate for accreditation by the Commission on Higher Education of the Middle States Association of colleges and schools in the US.

In the context of the choice of technologies from the Industrial Revolution or the Electronics Revolution, and the interface between group-based distance training or individual-based distance training, this development will be closely watched for:

- choice of technology
- previous failures to start an American distance university
- previous failures of the British Open University in the US
- failures of open universities in federal systems.

The OUUK is basically a print-based technology user, offering full degrees completely at a distance, for individual students. This contrasts with much of the US university distance learning scene today.

There have been many attempts to found an American distance university in the past. In the mid-1960s Dr Jerry Lord led a foundation in New York State. In 1982 the University of Mid-America at Lincoln, Nebraska, was disbanded. Many had seen it as an American open university but from the point of view of distance education theory it was structurally flawed. In 1999 a series of virtual universities failed to start, or failed to deliver on their hype. Many of these were political foundations ignoring the theory and practice of distance education.

The most notable previous attempt of the British Open University to enter the US market was the Open University Programme of University College of the University of Maryland at College Park. This was at its best in 1978, but the complexity of language of the OU materials, and the density of concepts, meant that they had to be largely rewritten for American sophomores and the initiative was later abandoned.

Federal education systems like the US, Canada, Germany, Australia and Brazil have poor records in founding a national open university. In Canada two small open universities, Athabasca in Alberta, and the TéléUniversité in Québec, have struggled to succeed outside their provincial boundaries. In Germany, the 1965 FIM project (*Fernstudium in Medienverbund*) was abandoned after 10 years of planning, when one of the ministers left the federal negotiations and founded one for his state. In Australia the 1973 Whitlam government's plans for an open university were thwarted by the states and the vested interests of existing providers, and never revived. Brazil has made a number of attempts in the 1990s to found an open university.

The future

Distance systems need to make decisions about the choice of technologies for distance training, and they need a view of the future based on what works and what fails in educating and training at a distance.

The influential 1979 Canadian study, *Gutenberg Two: The New Electronics and Social Change*, included a chapter which suggested that by 2004 Harvard University would be some type of distance training provider:

> Although Harvard no longer existed as a university campus since people could no longer afford the luxury of coming to one place for the sole purpose of learning and researching, the venerable name lingered on, having been acquired at some expense by a large publishing house. The 'Fellows' of Harvard were now scattered literally around the world.
>
> The original fellows had dissipated the endowment, first in publishing books with no hope of sale and finally, as an understanding of the future caught up with them, in rather stilted computer-aided learning routines. Unfortunately, they had not realised that in the meantime the population at large had ceased to be text literate but was instead image literate. That is, their understanding of the world around them was once more conditioned by images and sounds as had been the case with their distant ancestors. People just didn't read much anymore. (Godfrey *et al.* 1979:21–2)

The 1980s and early 1990s in the US saw the development of satellite systems for group-based distance training. These systems did not develop to the same extent in Europe. A satellite up-link in Europe costs $/€180,000 and it is unlikely that a European university would spend that money on distance students. Distance training in Europe remained largely individual-focused.

The early and mid-1990s in the US saw the development of videoconferencing systems for group-based distance training. These systems did not develop in Europe. A one-day training course in Europe (from Ireland to Sweden) at 384 kilobytes per second costs $/€1,824 in telephone costs alone. Distance training in Europe remained largely aimed at the individual student.

The mid- to late 1990s saw the development in the US of training on the WWW for individual-focused distance training in front of a computer screen. These systems were slower to develop in Europe, where minimal on-line access to the net can cost $/€1,500 per year in telephone costs alone.

The late 1990s and early 2000s see the introduction of mobile telephones and computers, the reduction of reliance on wiring, and, with the development of Bluetooth and other protocols, the growing empowerment of wirelessness. Of clear relevance to distance students and the future of distance learning, it may not have a similar impact on campus.

The mid-2000s seem to be indicated for the general availability of voice synthesis, voice recognition and voice input into telephones and computers, whether fixed or mobile. There should again be benefits for distance systems rather than on campus, because of the greater reliance of distance students on correspondence, assignment preparation, and assignment submission.

Conclusion

This chapter has identified tensions in technological innovation for the provision of qualifications to students who prefer to learn at a distance.

Far from seeing conflict in the tensions listed above, the vision here is of the richness and choice that confronts the learner in the twenty-first century for both education and training: schools, colleges and universities will continue to prosper, as will systems based on teaching at a distance. Teaching face-to-face at a distance in virtual and electronic systems will continue to prosper, as will training on the World Wide Web. To these will be added the boon of Bluetooth and mobile technologies, with the elimination of wiring and fixed installations for many applications, and the further benefit of voice input into machines.

3 Characteristics of distance training

Context

The aim of this chapter is to identify the strengths, weaknesses, and characteristics, of this sector of training provision with a view to evaluating its market in the twenty-first century.

Born in the nineteenth century, distance training came of age in the twentieth century, and went from strength to strength from 1970 to 2000, as the foundation of the open universities caused great improvements in both the quality and quantity of provision, and as the technologies of the new telecommunications industries were harnessed for training.

Distance training is often seen as a harbinger of the new millennium. To justify this role it needs to have been both a provider of training excellence in the twentieth century, and have characteristics that indicate a central training role in the twenty-first century.

Many of the themes that are key elements in government training policies in many countries at the dawn of the new millennium have been characteristics of distance training for decades:

- lifelong learning
- use of technology in training
- cost-effective provision
- the individualisation of training provision
- just-in-time training
- parity of esteem for men and women
- parity of esteem of further and higher education
- the globalisation of training.

It is considered that the characteristics identified here are to be found in both group-based and individual-based provision, though some of them may be attenuated as group-based provision moves nearer to conventional training, or to other forms of the use of technology for training. Few of the characteristics identified are shared by conventional provision, and few are centres of concern for open and/or flexible learning.

The characteristics identified are loosely grouped under four headings: societal, student-related, didactic and systemic.

Societal characteristics

Under this heading are grouped distance training for taxpayers, the globalising, individualising, industrialising roles of distance training, and its characterisation as the privatisation of institutional learning.

Training for taxpayers

Distance education is the education of taxpayers.

A very great part of each national education budget goes to the provision of:

- primary education
- secondary education
- government training centres
- colleges
- university undergraduates
- university postgraduates and doctorates.

But most of those who benefit from these structures do not pay taxes.

Government policies talk frequently about the provision of training for the long-term unemployed, the unemployed, the disabled, the early school dropouts, immigrants, and other special groups, but few of these pay taxes.

Taxpayers pay in full for all the groups listed above, but who pays for their education?

Taxpayers today have an urgent need for lifelong learning, for education and training, not just to get promotion and higher pay, but to keep their jobs.

If they do not keep their jobs they can't pay taxes for the education and training of society.

For over 100 years distance education has made a major contribution to the training of those in employment.

Distance education is largely the study of those who pay for their own training, and who also pay for the training of their fellow citizens with their taxes.

Conventional education is the study, in the main, of those who pay neither for their own training, nor for the training of those studying at a distance (who are paying for the conventional education from which they benefit).

Distance education is the study of those who do not travel to government training centres, to proprietary training centres, to schools, college or universities, often because they are in full-time employment.

The provision of training for taxpayers will be a central role for distance learning in the twenty-first century.

Globalisation

Distance education institutions have always had the potential to teach totally globally. For 100 years European distance education institutions, especially in Britain and France, have taught government and business cadres sent to their overseas territories, and frequently their children too. Thousands of government and business officers in Singapore, Nigeria, Hong Kong, Dakar, Abidjan and elsewhere, were trained at a distance.

In recent years, improvements in communications technologies have seen this possibility extended. Today the Centre National d'Enseignement à Distance (CNED) in Poitiers, France, enrols 36,000 of its students each year, in over 200 counties, and teaches them all over the world through to the level of competitive French examinations.

The development of e-mail has greatly enhanced these possibilities and student-to-institution communication via e-mail, institution-to-student-body communication by bulletin boards, and student-to-student communication via conferencing packages, are now features of many systems.

WWW-based courses offer distance education institutions further possibilities of developing their global offerings. Clusters of students on the web can work together on joint projects, though scattered all over the world. Teaching globally is rarely seen as a goal for flexible learning or for open learning with which distance training is sometimes confounded. It is a major asset in distance training's role in training in the twenty-first century.

Individualisation

The individualisation of teaching and learning is more marked in individual-based than in group-based distance provision, but both contain characteristics that distinguish it markedly and permanently from campus-based provision.

Conventional education in the East and West has always been characterised by face-to-face interaction between the teacher and the learner in the learning group. This leads inevitably to the problem of students of different abilities being in the same group.

From its outset in the middle of the nineteenth century, distance training broke the structure of the learning group and treated its students as individuals. In many cases an individual tutor, not a group-based teacher, was provided and it is claimed by scholars that frequently a creative one-to-one relationship was set up in the best distance teaching systems which had great benefits for learning.

It is now possible to measure students' entry characteristics, or reading abilities, or prior knowledge of the subject matter, and get the computer to punch out on paper, or on the web, a version of the course which has been individualised in response to the student data inputted.

The ability to individualise education and training is the trump card distance education holds in its role in lifelong learning in the twenty-first century.

Privatisation

Distance education is characterised by a privatisation of institutional teaching and a privatisation of institutional learning.

It thus corresponds to one of the fundamental societal trends in the West at the end of the second millennium: the privatisation of western society. This privatisation is most marked in countries where the sense of community has been replaced by a focus on the home.

Community activities like going to a restaurant are being replaced by the home barbecue; going to the theatre by watching the video; going to church is in decline; people are as likely to stay by their home pool as go to the seaside, and watch the match on television rather than go to the sports stadium. A distance system takes the student from the learning group and places him/her in a more private situation. Distance education is characterised by the privatisation of institutional learning.

Here is not the place to comment on whether the privatisation of education inherent in distance education is good or bad. This analysis underlines the appropriateness of the most privatised form of training for learning in a society facing rapid privatisation.

Further evidence for this trait can be found on the WWW. In spite of its e-mail, bulletin boards and conference packages, sitting alone in front of a computer screen is a very private way to study.

Industrialisation

The German scholar, Peters (1994), argued that it was no accident that distance education began in the middle of the nineteenth century in the areas of North America and Northern Europe most marked by the Industrial Revolution.

Peters claims that distance education is the most industrialised form of education and that all the teaching procedures of distance education can be paralleled in the industrial production of goods. Peters has produced a fruitful analysis that is quite foreign to the worlds of flexible learning or of open learning.

Today this contribution is still vigorously debated in the distance education literature: does it apply to very small systems? Does it apply to a society that, some say, is becoming post-industrialised? Does it apply to the group-based distance education systems of the US? Has it been superseded by the telecommunications developments of the 1980s?

Student-related characteristics

Here the characteristics of students who study at a distance because they wish to avoid study-related debt, or who are unable to attend institutions, or who have bad experiences of schooling, or who choose not to travel to study, or who refuse to attend schools, colleges or universities, are analysed.

Avoidance of debt

In the late 1990s eighteen-year-olds became a new market for distance training and distance university degrees. This market, created in the 1990s by changes in government policies in countries like the UK and the Netherlands, added to the low salaries paid to recent graduates in a range of professions, plus the widely accepted statistic that the average graduate emerges from university with a debt of €15,000.

'I wish I had gone to the OU straight from school because that way you can get a degree and build up your work experience at the same time', is a growing attitude. In practice many students at distance universities aged eighteen to twenty-one are financially supported by employers.

The reality of debt amongst the eighteen to twenty-one-year-olds who go to an ordinary university is only too well-known. Changes in government policy in the countries mentioned have changed the burden of payment for university from all the taxpayers of the country, to the student who enrols. There are now no grants, only loans. There are now contributory tuition fees as well as at least €3,000 each year for accommodation and food. In the UK a debt of £UK10,000 (€15,000) is regarded as average on completion of a degree programme at an ordinary university.

Students unable to travel or attend

Distance training is an important area of training provision because it is the *chosen* form of training for many millions of citizens per year. It is the *normal* form of training provision for many citizens who are isolated, for those who are too distant from the institution that provides the particular course they need, for those in full-time employment and for all who cannot meet the timetabling of lectures, classes, training sessions, practical or workshop sessions that are a characteristic of other forms of provision. It is the *only* form of provision for many prisoners, those who are hospitalised, disabled or disadvantaged, shift-workers and homemakers.

Changes have been made, it is true, in many schools, colleges and universities to accommodate blind students, deaf students, the severely disabled, and other handicapped students, but distance training provides an attractive alternative, by which disabled students can receive university degrees and training certification without the need to travel to venues on a regular basis.

Those who choose not to attend

This book analyses distance education and training. It does not promote it. In this context most of those who enrol in distance systems are seen as those who choose not to enrol in the schools, colleges and universities that society provides as the normal locations for the teaching/learning transaction to take place.

Thus the challenge for governments or ministries of education is to decide whether citizens are to be forced to go to the schools, colleges and universities which taxpayers' monies provide for their training, or whether governments should pay for them to study at a distance. As most of the distance students are taxpayers, who pay for the education of society by their taxes, are they to be forced out of the workforce so that they can accomplish their own training?

Those who refuse to travel

The individual-based forms of distance training provide a range of teaching/learning strategies, which vary with regard to face-to-face or electronic contact. Some systems have:

- no face-to-face contact
- voluntary face-to-face contact
- compulsory face-to-face contact.

Other systems have:

- no electronic contact
- voluntary electronic contact
- compulsory electronic contact.

This variety and flexibility of provision corresponds well to Bååth's maxim that there are four types of students who enrol in distance systems.

Students who need support and do not wish support	Students who need and wish support
Students who do not need but wish support	Students who do not need or wish support

Figure 3.1 Four types of distance training students
(Bååth 1980)

Group-based distance systems introduce some of the constraints of conventional colleges and universities: if the two-way audio, two-way videoconference meeting is at 14.00 in Toronto on a Tuesday:

- the student has to be there at that time, at that place, and not at work or at home;
- the institution has to pay for the construction, maintenance or leasing of the premises at which the videoconference is to take place.

In the late 1990s another factor developed that analysts must address: the refusal of students, especially women, especially at night, to travel to schools, colleges, training centres or universities for the purposes of instruction.

The safety of studying at home, as well as the convenience, will weigh heavily in favour of distance systems in the twenty-first century.

Those who have bad experience of education

Society provides schools, colleges and universities for the purposes of training. Many students, alas, fail.

Distance systems traditionally provide courses for adults at primary school level and at secondary school level. A major distance training market has always been matriculation, *Abitur*, HSC, 'O' Levels and 'A' levels at a distance, for adults who have not achieved high school graduation.

Distance education has traditionally been associated with second chance education, with the training of those who have been failed by the education system, whether at university or at college or at school level. It has also been a character-istic form of education for adults who dropped out of school early – and then found themselves without the basic levels of mathematics or English (or their corresponding national language) which are essential for holding down a job.

Finally, distance education and training is the usual form of training for those who have bad experiences and bad memories of school – those who never want to set foot in an educational establishment again. These people, too, need training and distance systems are the normal form of provision for them.

Didactic characteristics

Dimensions of distance systems are grouped here which affect both the students' learning possibilities and didactic choices by the institutions. The characteristics chosen for presentation here are feedback, didactic use of technology, mobility, lifelong learning and the World Wide Web.

Rapidity of feedback

Slowness of feedback used to be a characteristic of distance systems and a study by the Norwegian scholar, Rekkedal (1984), showed that turnaround time was a crucial variable in success or failure of distance learning.

The telecommunications revolution of the 1980s turned what was once a damaging characteristic to a potential trump card.

Today a distance education student can submit an assignment electronically from any place in the world, at any time of day or night, Christmas Eve or New Year's Day, and receive back immediately at any time of day or night, a personalised, customised feedback report indicating correct answers, analysing wrong answers, giving the student his or her grade, and offering advice on the next phase of study. Conventional colleges and universities usually take longer to return students' work.

Didactic use of technology

The separation of teacher and learner, and the learner from the learning group, means that distance training is always characterised by the didactic use of technology.

Some (Garrison 1985, Bates 1995) have suggested that distance training technologies should be grouped into generations. The position in this study is to show how the technologies of the Electronics Revolution (Duning 1993, Bramble 1996) have merged with previously available technologies, as distance training prepares for the more mobile technologies of the future.

Mobility

In the 1980s, it is said, the world went digital and distance systems responded with computer conferencing, two-way videoconferencing systems and teaching on the web.

At the present time the world is going mobile. Mobile phones and portable computers are replacing wired ones.

Distance training is well set up to meet the challenges of universal personal mobility and mobile internet access for courses, which will characterise communications in the immediate future. Flexible education and open learning are more suited to a wired environment. Some have argued that conventional universities will take over the provision of courses to distance students, but it is unlikely that the great universities throughout the world will pay much attention to the students who choose not to attend their campuses.

Unlike other systems, distance training can cope with the student who is not only at a distance, but is moving at a distance too. The concept of the award of university degrees to the student moving at a distance will challenge still further the concept of a university, and the skills of distance educators in designing quality learning systems.

First choice for lifelong learning

For over 100 years distance systems have been practising and providing lifelong learning.

The characteristics of the lifelong learning movement have been characteristics of distance systems for decades.

Distance systems have always been characterised by:

- freedom from the scheduling of classes
- freedom from space constraints
- freedom from time constraints
- freedom from joining learning groups in order to learn
- education for taxpayers
- education for homemakers
- education for the hospitalised, shift-workers, travellers, those in prison.

These characteristics which make distance training the first choice for lifelong learning are inherent in the nature of distance systems. Conventional systems, it is true, can be adapted to accommodate the characteristics of lifelong learners and taxpayers, by putting on their courses at night, or at remote locations, or at study centres, but if the lifelong learners refuse to travel to these locations, the programmes fail.

The theme of lifelong learning, much vaunted in the 1970s and the early 1980s, appears to be becoming more popular with governments and international development agencies. A form of educational provision that has maintained the characteristics of lifelong learning for 100 years, and in which the focus on these characteristics is an essential attribute of the form of provision, is a leading candidate for provision.

Didactic use of the WWW

The World Wide Web and corporate intranets give excellent services for teaching at a distance. It is now clear that students who already spend more than twenty hours a week in front of a computer screen, with web access, want to be trained on the web too (Fritsch 1997, 1998).

Unlike other forms of flexible training with which it is sometimes grouped, it is a characteristic of distance systems that they be available to web-based training, globally, with the student in this instance not moving from his or her screen for the purposes of training.

Collis (1996) has made a powerful case for the use of the web on campus too, but a very large part of web-based training will doubtless be at a distance.

Systemic characteristics

Systemic characteristics of distance systems are those which identify its role in national provision of education and training. These characteristics can have a crucial impact in combating the growing needs for training in both developing and developed countries alike. Chosen for presentation here are cost-effectiveness when compared with other forms of provision, ability to make a very large impact on national systems, the role of very large distance systems dealing competently with more than 100,000 students per year, rapid shifts in scale, and distance education as a professional field.

Cheaper than other forms of provision

Distance education and training quickly established itself as a cheaper form of educational provision. In a series of pertinent studies, Rumble (1997) showed that unless the investment in media was excessive, or the variable cost per student was higher than conventional systems, or the distance system could not attract sufficient students to warrant its investment in materials, the distance system would always be cheaper.

This was a great benefit to developing and developed countries alike, especially because they did not have to build buildings to house students.

Group-based distance systems erode these cost advantages because the investment in media can be high, the variable cost per student can be high, and student volumes tend to be lower. Buildings have to be built or rented for group-based systems. Daniel has vigorously restated the cost advantages of distance systems:

> The UKOU's costs are significantly lower than other institutions: between 39 per cent and 47 per cent of the other universities' costs for ordinary degrees; between 55 per cent and 80 per cent for honours degrees. Wagner in 1977 showed that the annual average recurrent cost per full-time undergraduate at the OUUK was less than one-third the cost at a campus university, and the cost of a UKOU graduate was less than half. Nearly 20 years later, Peters and Daniel, using a different type of analysis, showed that cost comparisons were still strongly in favour of the UKOU. (1996:39, 62)

Cost advantage will be a crucial factor in the choice of provision for the lifelong learner in the twenty-first century.

Very large systems

Work carried out in the late 1980s by the author showed that two distance systems, the CNED in France and the *Dianda* system in China, taught competently 1,000,000 students: the CNED had 400,000 and the *Dianda* system 600,000.

Coombs (1985) had shown that there was a world crisis in education owing to the rapid growth of learning needs and the growing financial squeeze on education resulting in rising unit costs and constrictive budget ceilings. It was clear that many countries needed very large education systems, which the author defined as systems which could competently teach an enrolment of 100,000 students per year.

Work carried on with UNESCO in the early 1990s (Keegan 1993) on the micro-didactics of megasystems showed that the very large distance systems like the CNED and the *Dianda* network with over 100,000 students could competently identify the study needs of their vast enrolments. Conventional systems like the University of Rome, La Sapienza, with 150,000 students in 1989, and the University of Madrid also with 150,000 in the late 1980s, had great difficulties – they could not build buildings for their vast student bodies and relied on a 20 per cent attendance rate.

Then, as now, the distance education systems with over 100,000 students form an important subset of provision and educational administrators and planners have pressing needs for the results of research on how such institutions behave, how they cope with their massive dispersed student bodies, their capital investment and annual recurrent costs, and their success or failure at the micro level in achieving academic excellence when compared with smaller systems both face-to-face and at a distance.

Countries differ in their choice of structure for the design of very large distance systems. In China the *Dianda* system comprises 44 open universities, one in each province, in each autonomous region, and each large municipality, at which the students are enrolled and attend the satellite lectures from Beijing. A number of the individual open universities are approaching the crucial 100,000 enrolments size.

In France the distance system is built up of layers of primary and secondary courses at a distance, vocational and further education courses at a distance, university and postgraduate courses at a distance, with responsibility for both developing materials and teaching students divided on a programme basis between the eight centres in different French cities (see Chapter 6). At the time of writing the CNED enrolment is divided almost equally between further and higher education provision.

Turkey, with over 600,000 students enrolled today at Anodolu University has followed another model with a small face-to-face university provision joined to a very large distance system (570,000) within the same university.

Other countries like India, Indonesia, Thailand, Korea, Iran, Spain, the UK, South Africa, have founded open universities, which demonstrate the inherent characteristic of distance systems to cope competently with very large student bodies of over 100,000 enrolments per year.

A listing of very large distance systems at the turn of the millennium with their dates of foundation and models can be found in Figure 3.2 opposite.

Very large distance systems can make excellent contributions to provision of education and training once they competently address the microdidactics of megasystems, that is the support and counselling of the individual student in the vast system.

Very large changes

Distance systems have the inherent characteristic of being able to vary their enrolment patterns in response to rapid changes in government or societal needs. They do not need to build buildings to take on an additional 10,000 students, nor are staffing needs as volume-sensitive as the problems that would face a government in placing an extra 10,000 students in a conventional college, university, or training centre.

In the mid-1990s both the Spanish UNED and the German Fernuniversität took on an extra 10,000 students in a short period of time due to rises in unemployment and changes in national training patterns. The inherent characteristic of distance systems to increase enrolment statistics in response to government and society's requirements is demonstrated by the history of the CNED in France (see Figure 3.3).

Very large impact

A distance system can make a unique impact on a national educational pattern as the statistics for the OUUK aptly show in Figure 3.4 on p. 33.

Institution	Country	Model	Date of foundation	Enrolment
Dianda	China	Network of universities	1979	600,000
Anadolu University	Turkey	Conventional university	1982	570,000
Charkov Beheer	Netherlands	Proprietary college	1990	450,000
CNED	France	Government institution	1939	405,000
Universitas Terbuka	Indonesia	Distance teaching university	1984	350,000
Indira Gandhi NOU	India	Distance teaching university	1985	250,000
Sukhothai Thammatirat OU	Thailand	Distance teaching university	1978	220,000
Korean NOU	South Korea	Distance teaching university	1982	200,000
UNED	Spain	Distance teaching university	1972	170,000
OUUK	UK	Distance teaching university	1969	165,000
UNISA	South Africa	Distance teaching university	1947	130,000
LOI	Netherlands	Proprietary college	1923	110,000
Payame Noor University	Iran	Distance teaching university	1987	110,000
CIDEAD	Spain	Government institution	1992	110,000

Figure 3.2 Distance systems with more than 100,000 enrolments 1999

1940	War years
1945	1,413
1950	8,300
1955	30,000
1960	61,000
1965	109,000
1970	146,000
1975	180,000
1980	197,000
1985	225,000
1990	250,000
1995	350,000
1999	403,000

Figure 3.3 Enrolment in the CNED 1939–99

The latest statistics published at the time of writing are for the 1998 intake, but it is clear that by the turn of the millennium over 1,500,000 citizens will have actually applied to do a university degree at a distance in a country with a population of less than 60,000,000.

A profession

The professionalisation of distance education is controversial. Scholars (Peters, Keegan) who hold that distance education is a form of educational provision see it as a professional field. Others who see it as only a mode of teaching, suggest that there is little difference between on-campus and off-campus teaching and that any competent academic or trainer can teach at a distance.

The first university degree in distance education to provide professional training in the field was developed for the University of South Australia (the former Adelaide College of Advanced Education) in 1982 and there have been a growing number of degrees and advanced qualifications both face-to-face and at a distance since then.

Year	Applications	Cumulative	Initial registration	Cumulative
1971	40,817	–	24,220	24,220
1972	34,222	75,039	20,501	44,721
1973	30,414	105,433	16,895	61,616
1974	34,017	139,470	14,976	76,592
1975	49,550	189,020	20,145	96,637
1976	51,450	240,470	17,159	113,796
1977	48,252	288,722	20,097	133,893
1978	42,833	331,555	21,000	154,893
1979	40,235	371,790	21,140	176,033
1980	45,125	419,444	19,448	195,481
1981	42,373	461,817	20,332	214,813
1982	45,667	507,484	25,311	241,124
1983	43,332	550,816	25,613	266,737
1984	41,495	592,311	21,591	288,328
1985	49,691	642,002	19,366	307,694
1986	56,077	698,079	20,147	327,861
1987	56,820	754,899	22,416	350,277
1988	59,336	814,235	25,041	375,318
1989	56,314	870,549	23,023	398,341
1990	54,852	925,401	24,240	422,851
1991	62,989	988,390	25,164	447,745
1992	68,109	1,056,499	27,608	475,353
1993	63,054	1,119,553	29,527	564,880
1994	67,467	1,187,020	33,612	538,492
1995	65,471	1,252,491	36,082	574,574
1996	63,145	1,315,636	35,915	610,489
1997	69,242	1,384,878	37,279	647,768
1998	72,828	1,457,706	41,086	688,854

Figure 3.4 Cumulative enrolments in the OUUK 1971–99

4   Virtual and distance training

Context

> Not long ago we all wished that the world would take more interest in what
> we did and show more appreciation of the virtues of distance learning. Today
> we must often wish we could be released from the close embrace of Wall
> Street, the technology companies, and the media. With a guru like Peter
> Drucker announcing the imminent demise of campus education, right-thinking
> people have suddenly discovered how important distance learning is. Where
> were they when we needed them? (Daniel 1999)

Is the field of distance learning ready to take centre stage? Unfortunately for those
who promote it, there are many indications that this is not so. Its theoretical
underpinnings remain unacceptably fragile. Its institutions seem naive in protecting
their vast market from predators. Its open universities have so far failed to convince
in their research contributions to the theory and practice of distance education. Few
rules have been established to evaluate the didactic value of each new information
and communication technology as it appears.

There is still confusion as to what is included within the terms *distance
education*, *distance learning* or *distance training* and what is excluded by them.
Terms like *virtual learning* or *web-based training* or *courses on the internet* or
technology-based training are introduced without precision. Terms like *flexible
learning* or *distributed learning* or *open learning* or *ODL* or even *open-distance
learning* come and go.

Discourtesy to the reader is the result of this lack of precision, and lack of
progress in distance education research.

In this book, distance education and training are considered a discrete sector
of educational provision, with its own rules and characteristics, which mark it
out from other sectors of provision. It is also regarded as a field of research
within the discipline normally referred to as 'education' and on a par with other
fields of educational research like comparative education, or educational psychology, or educational technology, or adult education (Amundsen and Collinge
1999).

In the use of terminology it is considered that the American association
of distance colleges, the Distance Education and Training Council (DETC) of

Washington DC, has got it right. Its name aptly reflects the field because its members offer courses both for further education awards at a distance, and for higher education awards at a distance.

The terms *distance education* and *distance training* correspond to the distinctions between further education and higher education. Thus, further education at a distance is generally referred to in this book as *distance training*, and higher education at a distance as *university-level distance education* or simply *distance education*.

Distance training

Global statistics show that at least 70 per cent of distance provision for adults is at further education level rather than higher education. This accurately reflects the linking of distance systems to the working adult or the adult seeking employment, or to training for the taxpayer or for persons in full-time employment, who frequently need training and upgrading for vocational purposes, but not necessarily at university degree level

Schreiber and Berge's *Distance Training. How Innovative Organisations Are Using Technology to Maximise Learning and Meet Business Objectives* (1998) provides a useful companion volume to the present work because it deals with the use of distance training within American business corporations, whereas this book deals only with programmes which are available at a distance to the public in general.

Schreiber and Berge build up their book from 16 case studies taken from US business, non-profit organisations, and government agencies and conclude that 'there is an ever-increasing explosion of interest now in corporate video-conferencing, electronic performance support systems, and online web-based courses by companies and industry' (1998: XV).

This approach contrasts with the census approach followed in this book. It was felt that case studies are too ephemeral and date too quickly for the state-of-the-art overview and stocktaking aimed at here.

Placing side by side the mainly in-house, distance training of corporations, of Schreiber and Berge, with the provision of courses for the public by government and proprietary institutions in this study, the distance training industry can be adequately presented.

Distance education

Distance education is used in this book in its legal sense for the provision, either public or private, of education and training for nationally-recognised degrees, diplomas and certificates, to students who choose not to, or who are unable to, or who refuse to, attend the schools, the colleges, and the universities, which society provides for the purposes of learning.

Clearly the choice of terminology like 'students who refuse to go to college' is that of the analyst or the stocktaker, and would not be used by stakeholders who choose to champion distance learning or criticise campus universities.

There will always be a need for a term to characterise the sector of education which offers educational qualifications to those students who do not attend educational institutions, and it seems appropriate to use the well-established term *distance education* for this sector, whether the provision is made electronically or not.

Besides these legal dimensions, the study is based on a previously published definition (Keegan, 1996, p. 50):

Distance education is a form of education characterised by:

- The quasi-permanent separation of teacher and learner throughout the length of the learning process (this distinguishes it from conventional face-to-face education);
- The influence of an educational organisation both in the planning and preparation of learning materials and in the provision of student support services (this distinguishes it from private study and teach-yourself programmes);
- The use of technical media – print, audio, video or computer, or the World Wide Web, to unite teacher and learner and carry the content of the course;
- The provision of two-way communication so that the student may benefit from or even initiate dialogue (this distinguishes it from other uses of technology in education); and
- The quasi-permanent absence of the learning group throughout the length of the learning process so that people are usually taught as individuals rather than in groups, with the possibility of meetings, either face-to-face or by electronic means, for both didactic and socialisation purposes.

The World Bank web site has a glossary of distance education terms at http://wbweb4.worldbank.org/Distant/glossary.html, which gives shorter definitions:

Distance education: Teaching and learning in which learning normally occurs in a different place from teaching.

Distance learning: Term often used as synonymous with distance education, not strictly correctly since distance education includes teaching as well as learning.

The question raised by these concepts for the analyst is that society has for some hundreds, if not thousands, of years provided itself with locations called schools, and higher level locations called universities, at which the teaching–learning interaction takes place. The question for the analyst is whether institutional learning is essentially linked to these privileged places for institutional learning created by society.

Distance education students choose to remain in employment, at home with their families. They refuse to give up their jobs to study. They expect to be given institutional learning at home and, more and more frequently as the new millennium starts, to be able to study for university degrees at home, isolated in front of a screen. The ideas of Von Humboldt, or Arnold, or Newman that universities are places where students come together for the purposes of learning, do not convince them to travel to colleges or to reside at them.

The problem of the location of the student is a crucial one for the analyst. Clearly the conception and definitional precision given above can be attenuated by grouping distance students. In the Chinese *Dianda* system and in some of the distance learning structures in the US, students sit in front of videoconference screens, or satellite-linked television screens, which may be 10km or 1,000km from the university awarding the degree. Distance students can be clustered together electronically on the web to work on joint projects.

Education and training

What is the difference between education and training, whether face-to-face, or at a distance, or on the web?

From the point of view of businesses, training is usually viewed as being job-specific or related to one's current job as in on-the-job-training or just-in-time training. Training is of value to the business to which the employee belongs in the short term, say over two or three years. Training deals with activities that can be seen by management as being in the best interest of the organisation.

Education, on the other hand, has a broader scope and less relationship to the current job. Education tends to improve the longer-term value of the person, who will then be of greater value to the corporation, but not necessarily in the next few years.

It is nevertheless true that no education or training course is all one or all the other. Every training programme has an element of education in it, and most educational programmes have effects and dimensions that fall within training.

Schreiber and Berge's book highlights the fact that distance training played a larger and larger role in in-house company and corporation training in the 1990s. Examples are:

- In the early 1990s, IBM launched their international satellite education network (ISEN), providing training for employees who came together in IBM education centres all over America.
- In the mid-1990s Deutsche Telekom installed dedicated videoconferencing for training its employees throughout Germany.
- In the late 1990s many corporations put their training programmes on the web, providing virtual training centres or their own virtual universities.
- The Microsoft CTEC training accreditation and certification became a new industry standard for courses in computing science, providing qualifications as valuable as those offered by public providers.

In this study, parity of esteem is accorded to both training and education at a distance. It is acknowledged that distance training has always been the major focus in distance provision, with further education enrolments easily outranking higher education enrolments. The book deals equally with vocational provision to citizens, whether provided by university level structures or not.

Distributed learning

Distributed learning is a dominant term in this field at the time of writing, perhaps the dominant term for many.

This will come as a shock to many who do not use it, especially those whose first language is not English, and distance education trainers and practitioners in Europe, Australia, and even Canada, who may not be familiar with the term, and do not realise that it is important in their field.

A major thread of discussion in the electronic literature in 1999 focused on 'distributed learning versus distance learning', or 'distributed learning versus distance education'.

These contributions claimed, in general, that *distance education* and *distributed education* were related, but that the 'distributed branch of the family had its roots in e-mail and teleconferencing, whereas *distance education* had the postal service and television as its ancestors'.

In this study, learning is a neural process that occurs in the minds of learners, whether they study in a face-to-face or distance system, or learn by themselves. It cannot be distributed. It is important to underline, however, the importance for distance educators of realising that for many in the US *distributed learning* is a normal nomenclature for what they do all day long.

Distance learning

An AltaVista search on the internet at the turn of the millennium brought:

- 203,906 hits for the term 'distance learning'.
- 118,223 hits for the term 'distance education'.
- 27, 485 hits for the term 'open learning' and
- 1,732 hits for the term 'open education'.

Thus 'distance learning' is by far the most-used term on the web for describing the field of education referred to as 'distance training' in this book.

Distance learning has a major organisation, the United States Distance Learning Association (USDLA), comprising major US universities and major US business corporations, to promote and develop its interests.

'Distance learning' in these contexts refers to three modes of distance training provision:

- the American satellite-based mode
- the American videoconferencing-based mode
- training on the World Wide Web.

As the term is not used in this way in other parts of the world, it is important to spell out what *distance learning* means: a professor in a US university gives his or her lecture face-to-face to the normal on-campus students in the normal lecture theatre. The lecture is then either beamed out live by satellite to groupings of students brought together at other locations, or is recorded on videotape and transmitted later to students who download it from the satellite, for either live viewing or for studying at a later date at their convenience.

In a similar way, distance learning is the mode of provision using video-conferencing adopted by US military training, US universities and colleges, or US corporations, in which, for example, a lecturer at a central US college or military academy teaches live at a distance, to a group of students at a remote location, or groups of students at remote locations.

This harnessing of the technologies of the Electronics Revolution to distance learning has led seamlessly to provision over the web, so that the term *distance learning* today encompasses training by satellite, training by videoconferencing, and training on the web.

Provision in the Chinese *Dianda* system has parallels with distance learning in the US, as students are brought together at workplace study centres all over China with their tutors, to follow lectures beamed out live by satellite from the Central Chinese Radio and TV University in Beijing.

Government officials and distance education researchers in Europe, and elsewhere, may protest and state that this is not what they understand by 'distance learning' at all. For them distance learning is an individual-based form of provision, usually used synonymously with 'distance education'. It is seen as a popular term for individual study at a distance, because it is perceived as a more student-centred term and more suitable for attracting government funding. The frequency of the term 'distance learning' on the web is such, however, that the claims of group-based provision to the term cannot be denied.

Virtual learning

Paulsen at http://www.nettskolen.com/kurs.html (1/12/99) describes on-line education: 'There are many terms for on-line education, some of them are: virtual education, internet-based education, web-based education, and education via computer-mediated communication.'

Today virtual education is represented by a growing number of virtual universities on the web, including virtual universities of open universities and virtual universities of multinational corporations, which are rapidly developing into a vibrant sector (see Chapters 9 and 10).

A virtual training system comprises an electronic classroom from which the class is taught, a network of specially-equipped electronic classrooms at which the students are present, and the satellite, microwave or cable linkups between them. For teaching purposes virtual classrooms can be either two-way video, two-way audio systems, often called videoconferencing, or one-way video with two-way audio, in which the lecturer cannot see the remote students, but feedback for them is provided by a telephone hook-up.

'Do virtual learners teach themselves?' was a thread in didactic discussions in 1999. Many of the contributions to discussion on this theme evoke a cognitivist philosophy of educational communication, in which it is claimed that the teacher is reduced to the role of a facilitator, and the virtual students actively construct their own courses, do their own research, choose their own evaluation criteria, and follow hyper-linked materials according to their own entry level established by diagnostic tests.

This contrasts with the view of learning as a reciprocal process between teacher and learner in which the teacher's role is the selection of the volume of course content, from the amount of information available, which is then designed by the teacher to meet the training needs of the student group enrolled for the level of certification desired. As the volume of information increases, as it did on most topics during the 1990s, the role of the teacher becomes more and more crucial in this viewpoint.

Students today are faced with the vastness of information on almost every subject which is available on the web. More so than previously, therefore, students may require the teacher to design the boundaries of the field of study, and to select from the data available precisely those elements which are relevant to the level of certification for the particular course they have chosen.

Web-based learning

There is now little doubt that the World Wide Web is the most successful educational tool to have appeared in a long time.

As recently as 1995 the first course offerings were venturing on to the internet, often consisting of materials delivered on paper with access to an e-mail package. By 1996 the first course materials were being designed for the web. In 1997 virtual universities, virtual campuses and virtual training centres were springing up all over the web. By 1998 web-based learning was a mature field of educational endeavour (see Chapter 9) with administrators speaking with experience of their systems tracking 10,000 students on the web.

This study takes the position that web-based training is a new field of distance training and that there are seamless interfaces between distance education and web-based training. It regards training on the World Wide Web as an electronic form of distance training, and claims that the laws and the rules, such as they are, that have been developed for distance education course development strategies, and student support services provision, and the logistics of the administration of distance systems, will transfer *mutatis mutandis* to provision on the World Wide Web.

What is excluded?

Certain forms of training at a distance are not the subject of the analysis of this book; they are left for other researchers.

The book has a precise focus on the professional and vocational training of adults at a distance, and studies only those courses which are available to the general public. Training is interpreted broadly to include any programme that would contribute to career advancement.

Three major areas of distance training are therefore excluded from consideration.

The first of these is the provision of courses at a distance for children. This is a large field with achievements throughout the twentieth century and is a subject in its own right.

In like manner, the whole area of corporate distance training, training on firewalled intranets, and in-house staff training at a distance is excluded from this study.

Finally, hobby courses like Flower Arranging or courses for similar interests at a distance, are not part of this analysis.

Census study

The study is based on a census of distance training provision in the European Union at the end of the 1990s. This was an exercise in state-of-the-art evaluation, in the provision of a market observatory, and in stocktaking at a time of transition.

As in all studies of this kind, precision and accuracy are the perequisites and generalisations, projections or estimates are not admissible. The phenomenon that is the subject of the census must be countable, otherwise the stocktaking cannot proceed.

It is considered that distance training as an educational phenomenon is measurable and countable when the definition developed in *Foundations of Distance Education* (Keegan), and widely commented on in the literature (Garrison and Shale 1987), is used as a defining instrument. It is considered that, in nearly every case, using this formula one can decide which forms of training provision are to be considered part of the census and which forms are not.

For this reason, a range of other forms of professional and vocational training for adults, which some may see as similar to, or identical with, or as sharing some of the same goals as distance training, are not included in this study, and are regarded as the work of other scholars. These include flexible learning, open learning, open and distance learning (ODL) and open distance learning.

Flexible learning

The term flexible learning has been used in government policy documents since the early 1990s and is an important goal for programmes today. In her *Flexible and Distance Learning*, Van den Brande supports the term and provides this explanation:

> Flexible learning is enabling learners to learn when they want (frequency, timing, duration), how they want (modes of learning), and what they want (that is learners can define what constitutes learning to them). These

flexible learning principles may be applied at a distance. If so then the term 'distance learning' is used. In such courses the learners can choose where they want to learn (at home, at an institution or company, at a training centre, etc. (1993:2)

At the time of writing flexible learning is used widely in the UK and in Australia where flexible learning centres have replaced open learning centres.

In this book flexible learning is considered a social learning goal. As the new century dawns flexible learning is a goal for all learners whether on-campus or off-campus. It is, therefore, considered not measurable in statistical terms and unsuitable as a generic term for the field of educational endeavour studied in this book.

Open learning

The term 'open learning' is now in widespread use in Europe and Australia and some explanation is needed for why it is not used in this book.

A basic reason is that it is not countable.

Opinions differ on what is 'open' and the same structure can be considered open by some and closed by others. Plato, for instance, is considered by educational historians to have developed an open, dialogic educational methodology but was castigated for being 'closed' by the German epistemologist, Popper, in his *The Open Society and Its Enemies* (1964).

Open learning is a goal for which all learners strive whether on-campus or off-campus and is the subject of other studies.

Reasons for not using it here include:

* The *distance* training colleges, like Bestuur Afstandsonderwijs (see Chapter 6) for example, could be considered more open than many *open* learning programmes. They are open to enrolment at any time, they are open to all as they do not charge fees, they are open to students to finish in their own time, they do not have closed cut-off dates for tutor-marked assignments (TMAs) and computer-marked assignments (CMAs).
* Open learning has less of the characteristics of distance training systems outlined in Chapter 3.
* In the late 1990s distance learning is vastly present on the internet in a way that does not apply to open learning.
* The cognate terms 'open education' and 'open teaching' have received little support.

In any case, distance training programmes are essentially both open and closed. They are open because they free the citizen from the necessity of travelling to an institution on a fixed schedule; they are closed because the course developers close off other views or interpretations besides the one closed for presentation. Distance training is just a form of educational provision. It is quite neutral. Some courses are open, some are closed, *per se* it is neither.

It is felt therefore that open learning and distance training can be adequately distinguished in spite of the practice of blurring the distinctions between them.

ODL

ODL or open and distance learning is a term used extensively in European Commission documentation.

It is considered here that open and distance learning is an unfortunate mixture which groups programmes and systems with disparate goals, and leads to vagueness and confusion in the distance training industry market.

Much greater synergies can be found between 'open and flexible learning', on the one hand, for programmes that have different ideals and characteristics to those outlined in Chapter 3, and between 'virtual and distance training', on the other hand, for those that do.

Open distance learning

This term is regarded as a mis-translation, a form of Brusselspeak.

Investigation by the author has shown that a document, prepared for a Brussels committee by the well-known Dutch distance educator, de Vocht, used the term '*open Afstandsonderwijs*' which means 'Distance education programmes for which normal entry requirements have been waived' but was mistranslated into English as 'open distance learning'. This expression possibly means in English 'non-closed distance learning'. Although some see 'non-closed' as a criticism of the lack of student-centredness in certain courses at a distance, the term is best regarded as a mistake and should be abandoned.

Happily, there has been little adoption of this European Commission term in the literature of distance education from Canada, Australia, the US and New Zealand, the major non-European contributors to the literature of distance education in English. By the time of writing, it appeared that the European Commission authorities were no longer supporting the use of the term.

Conclusion

This chapter has identified present and future stakeholders in this and related fields.

It identifies two clusters of stakeholders and shows the legal and contractual differences between them. The virtual training and distance training cluster, and the subject of this book, embraces programmes for nationally and internationally accepted degrees and diplomas and certificates for students who legally and contractually do not reside at, or travel to, or attend in any contractual manner commensurate with the degree to be awarded, the training centres or colleges or universities providing the award. The institutional structures may be electronic, or non-electronic, or a combination of both.

The flexible learning and open learning cluster, and the subject of other studies, groups programmes for students who, either corporately or individually, are enrolled in award-granting colleges or universities, but for whom more open and more flexible patterns or schedules are permitted.

Distance training is seen as a form of provision which purports to provide a complete educational and training system, from application to examination and certification (often many years later), parallel to and complementary to the normal face-to-face, group-based provision of vocational education and training.

5 The distance training models and their future

Overview

An overview of the field of distance training was provided in Chapter 1. It brought together data from the US, from China, from Europe, and from the rest of the world, especially Australia, Asia, South America and the rest of North America.

In this overview, all distance training systems at the dawn of the third millennium, were classified into four systems:

- Systems for groupings of full-time students
- Systems for groupings of part-time students
- Systems for individuals with pre-prepared materials
- Systems for individuals without pre-prepared materials.

The goal was to provide the reader with an accurate and up-to-date view of this whole sector of educational endeavour and field of educational research.

Valuable as such presentations of whole sectors may be, the richness and complexity of the field require more detailed analysis. The next stage is to establish reliable data on the institutional providers.

To achieve the accuracy required for taking stock of the strengths and weaknesses of the sector, it was clearly necessary to count all the institutions in a given area. Equally clearly, it was impossible to count all the institutional providers in all countries of the world.

As a large and representative sample of provision it was decided to count all European distance training providers, and more precisely all providers in the 15 nations of the EU operating in the year leading up to 1 January 2000.

Results

No fewer than 874 institutional providers were identified.

Although this is an impressive figure for the reader, and for the stocktaker, it poses further problems of analysis.

The 874 institutions are so disparate that it would be almost impossible to make meaningful general statements about their training provision. A classification or typology of the 874 institutions was needed so that models of provision could be delineated and the stakeholders identified.

In what follows, criteria for the delineation of a valid typology are provided, and this typology is applied to the 874 institutions identified in the countries chosen.

These rules for the construction of a valid typology are accepted here:

- It should be helpful to readers, enabling them to focus on a range of institutions within the field, 'distance teaching institutions', about which statements can be made that identify what this grouping of institutions has in common, and what it is that distinguishes it from the other groupings.
- To be helpful it should not be artificial – each grouping should contain a number of institutions.
- It should not be artificial with regard to students – each grouping should enrol thousands, preferably millions, of students.
- It should not be artificial with regard to time – each grouping should have been identifiable for at least a decade, preferably longer.
- It should try to encompass all distance teaching institutions, public and private, and not just concentrate on distance education at university level.
- It should only include those distance teaching institutions or departments of existing institutions which exhibit both the major characteristic subsystems of distance institutions (course development and student support services).

In the light of these guidelines, there are four models of provision of distance training at the turn of the millennium in the EU, and it is considered that these are mirrored elsewhere. The four models are:

- The government distance training institution
- The proprietary distance training institution
- The distance teaching university
- Distance education courses from a university.

In the EU there are four examples of model one, many hundreds of examples of model two, seven examples of model three and some hundreds of examples, with various sub-models, of model four. Each of the four institutional models identified has been established for decades and has enrolled many millions of students.

Model 1   Government distance training institutions

This is a well-established model of which the Centre National d'Enseignement à Distance (CNED), founded in France in 1939, and the Open Polytechnic of New Zealand, founded at Lower Hutt in 1946, are major examples.

The invasion of France led to the creation of the Centre National d'Enseignement par Correspondance (CNEC) by a government decree of 2 December 1939 to meet the needs of school children dislocated by war. In the mid-1980s the name was changed to its present form, CNED, which might be translated as National Centre for Distance Teaching.

The New Zealand Open Polytechnic today operates from a former girls' school in a quiet corner of Lower Hutt with support from a number of regional resource centres. Unlike other polytechnics and universities, it 'belongs' to no particular city or region but rather to the country as a whole, and hardly any of the hundreds of thousands of students who have studied with the Open Polytechnic over the years have ever set foot on its premises.

The characteristics of this model, the government distance training college, together with the listing of the government institutions worldwide which comprise it are:

- many of the foundations made in or after World War II
- full-time specialist staff for course development at all levels in their discipline
- full-time specialist staff for student support services
- heavy investment in plant, printing machinery, audio studios, video studios, or access to government plant
- capable of enrolling tens of thousands, or hundreds of thousands of students
- great economies of scale
- great economies of scope
- same production staff for courses at all levels
- possibility of multilevel provision at secondary, training, further, higher, and university levels.

A graphical representation of the didactic and administrative structures of institutions in this model is provided in Figure 5.1.

The model is well-established in many parts of the world and a listing of these government institutions with their dates of foundation and original titles (as many have changed their names in the 1990s) would include:

1 New South Wales Open Training and Education Network (OTEN), formerly the New South Wales College of External Studies, Sydney, Australia, claimed to go back to the New South Wales Correspondence Teaching Division in 1909.
2 Centre National d'Enseignement à Distance (CNED), Poitiers, France, formerly the Centre National de Télé-enseignement (CNTE), originally the Centre National d'Enseignement par Correspondance (CNEC), 1939.
3 The Open Polytechnic of New Zealand at Lower Hutt, formerly the New Zealand Technical Correspondence Institute/School, 1946.
4 Queensland Open Learning Network, Brisbane, Australia, formerly the Queensland College of External Studies, 1946.
5 South Australian College of External Studies (1947), Adelaide, Australia, later the South Australian Open College of Further Education, today remodelled.
6 Royal Melbourne Institute of Technology External Studies Department (1948), Australia, later the Victorian TAFE (Technical and Further Education) Off-campus Network, today remodelled.
7 Western Australian Technical Extension Service (1949), Perth, Australia, today remodelled.

8 Enseignement à distance de la Communauté Française de Belgique (1959), Brussels, Belgium, formerly Le Service des cours par correspondance de l'Etat (Belgique).

9 Bestuur Afstandsonderwijs (1959), Brussels, Belgium, formerly as above.

10 National Extension College (1963) Cambridge, UK, included here as a forerunner of UK government initiatives like the Open University, the Open Tech, the Open College of the Air, the Open Polytechnic. It is a limited company charity.

11 Centro para la Inovación y Desarrollo de la Educación a Distancia (CIDEAD) (1992), Madrid, Spain, incorporating some of the roles of INEM (Instituto Nacional de Educación Com Medias) (1968).

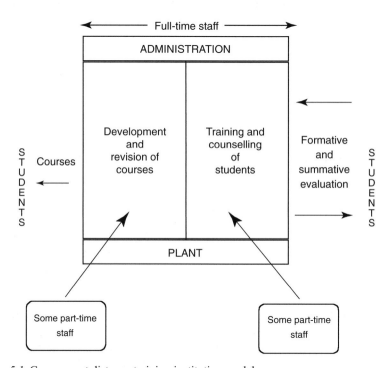

Figure 5.1 Government distance training institution model

The institutions in this model are specially-structured government institutions for distance training, with full-time staff engaged both in the development of courses for students at a distance, and in providing two-way communication and support services for students studying at a distance.

They have for decades taught hundreds of thousands of students annually, but because they are government institutions working mainly at further education level, there has been little appreciation in the literature of their contribution to distance education.

Model 2 Proprietary distance training colleges

Some would trace this model back 150 years to the middle of the nineteenth century, but it has been argued that institutions that exhibit all the characteristics of the rigorous definition of distance training adopted in this study do not predate the 1870s.

The model may be characterised as an institutional structure whose didactics are frequently patterned thus: the colleges develop or purchase learning materials and send them by post to the student. The student studies the materials and posts assignments back to the institution which marks and comments on them and posts them back to the student. The student studies the comments, completes the next assignment and the process is repeated.

A graphical presentation of the didactic and administrative structures of institutions in this model is provided in Figure 5.2.

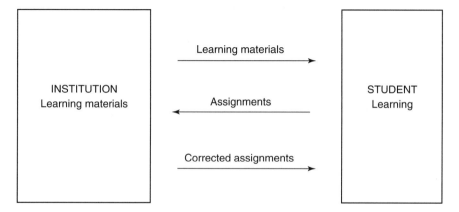

Figure 5.2 Proprietary distance training college model

The students' main contact with the representatives of the college is by post, telephone or e-mail so that isolation can be a problem. There are, nevertheless, institutions which have turned these disadvantages into factors which benefit student learning. There is evidence (Bååth 1980) to claim that the correspondence tutor can forge with the distant student a form of privileged one-to-one study that is difficult to create in a lecture or tutorial.

In the EU in recent years some of these colleges, especially in the Netherlands, have moved to university level courses and introduced state-of-the-art technologies.

This is a group of providers which has received little attention in the distance education literature because of its proprietary character.

There are many hundreds of institutions of this model in the EU today, ranging from Leidse Onderwijsinstellingen in the Netherlands with over 100,000 students enrolled, to small colleges with a few hundred enrolments or less.

Model 3   Distance teaching universities

Fernuniversitäten, Universidades de Educación a Distancia, or Open Universities are examples of a model with a long history. Although the normal name in English for distance teaching universities is 'open university' the term 'distance teaching university' is more generic and better translates 'Fernuniversität' and 'Universidad de Educación a Distancia' and so is adopted here.

Peters (1994) gives 1929 as the date of foundation of the first distance teaching university in the, then, Soviet Union and lists the 18 Soviet distance teaching universities with their faculties and enrolments in the early 1960s. Other foundations followed in the, then, Union of South Africa in 1947, and in China in 1960. A new series of universities teaching at a distance commenced with the UK's Open University in 1969.

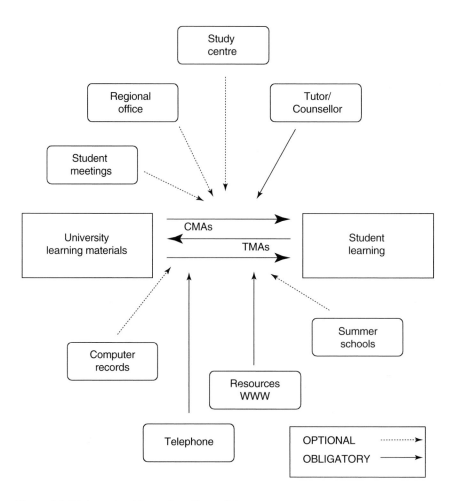

Figure 5.3 Distance teaching university model

The importance of the institutions in this model is that they provide specialist distance education courses and support systems for students at university level and provide governments with structures for coping competently with very large student bodies.

Recent foundations include the Open University of Tanzania (1994), the Virtual University of Catalonia (1995), the Open University of Bangladesh (1996), and the Hellenic Open University in Greece in 1997.

A graphical presentation of the didactic and administrative structures of universities in this model is provided in Figure 5.3 (see p. 50).

Model 4   Distance education courses from a university

This again is not a new model and historians give varying dates of 1873 (Bloomington), or 1875 (Ithaca), or 1892 (Chicago) for the first instances in the US.

Today the model is the usual form of university provision at a distance in many EU countries, especially Finland, Sweden, France, the UK, Ireland, Belgium – in fact most of the countries that have chosen not to found an open university.

The characteristics of this model are that course development is usually by university faculty (paid overload to produce the courses) or by consultants, and tuition is also provided by the university faculty or tutors hired by the department. The students study for degrees or certificates awarded by the university. Although there are a range of submodels the model might be represented diagrammatically thus:

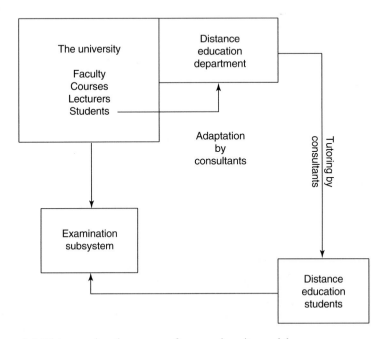

Figure 5.4 Distance education courses from a university model

There are various submodels of the ways in which a distance education programme is organised within a university. Distance education may be handled either by:

- a small department (as in a number of French universities)
- a special department of distance education (University of Florida at Gainesville)
- an integrated mode in which the full-time faculty teach equally both face-to-face and at a distance (University of New England, Australia)
- distance students being taught directly by the normal faculty (Sheffield Hallam University, UK).

The models in the EU 2000

The data presented in Chapter 12 shows the distribution of the models in the EU as:

Government distance training	4
Proprietary distance institutions	650
Distance teaching universities	7
Conventional universities	213
Total	*874*

Figure 5.5 Models in the EU 1999

In the compilation of these statistics the normal distinction between further and higher education is used, but with the proviso that parity of esteem between further education and higher education at a distance is accepted.

Very little synergy between the four models of distance training provision was found in the data. It is possible, in the same country in the EU, for an MBA (Masters in Business Administration) programme in Business Management, or a course in accountancy, to be offered by an institution representing each of the four categories.

The challenge for the four models today is how to protect and develop their share of the market.

The future

So much data has been compiled about these institutions and their models that it is believed that the phenomenon of distance training, as defined, has been subjected to a census so precise, that, in general, phenomena do not exist that could seriously modify the data.

Unlike other research methodologies, a census study leaves little room for surprises. In this context the reader may expect some guidance on the models of the future. In what follows seven scenarios are considered: the continuance of the four models identified as dominant at the end of the twentieth century and new possibilities which may emerge in the twenty-first: the corporate sector model; the World Wide Web model; the global provision model.

1   The government training institution model

Two of the institutions, the CNED, in France, and the Open Polytechnic, in New Zealand, have gone from strength to strength. The CNED with 405,000 students enrolled in the year 2000, is Europe's largest training provider, whether face-to-face or at a distance. In a similar way, the Open Polytechnic, in New Zealand, has embraced not only further education at a distance, but also the higher education sector and established itself as a major provider.

The other European institutions in Spain and in Belgium appear to have come through periods of analysis at the end of the 1990s with success, and seem to be on a safe road to the future. The Australian models, on the other hand, have all been merged, or reduced in importance, and this reaction by government is a warning to the other members of this group of what can happen if they do not defend their market.

2   The proprietary distance education model

The path to the future here is very varied. It is clear from the data already available, that, in Spain, the proprietary institutions are holding their own, in Germany and the Netherlands they appear to be reasonably stable, but in other parts of Europe, particularly France and Scandinavia, this model has seen its enrolment greatly reduced in the 1990s.

There are two reasons for this. One is the declining market for the 'correspondence' image. The other is government hostility to private provision in a number of countries, or the hostility of government-funded institutions. The future seems to be, to embrace a more electronic form of distance provision, and to be aware that if the multinational proprietary in-house providers enter the general market, they will pose a major threat to this sector.

3   The open universities

The open university is now a model which is available worldwide, with over 40 examples in China, and at least as many in the rest of the world. These institutions went through a difficult period in the 1980s, when critics labelled them as 'monolithic' and unable to hold their segment of the market. In the 1990s, on the other hand, there seemed to be a renewed confidence and competence among the open universities, which augurs well for the twenty-first century.

4 The provision of distance education from a university

Again, this is a model with a varied future. Clearly, it is the standard model in those countries which have chosen not to found an open university and, clearly, many universities will teach students on the World Wide Web in the twenty-first century. The achievement of academic excellence by the OUUK, in rankings provided by the UK government, however, which showed that many universities competing for the distance university market in the UK, with small departments and poorly-funded staff, could not compete with the Open University when teaching face-to-face, let alone at a distance, has raised questions about quality control. (See Chapter 7.)

5 The corporate sector in-house training model

The in-house provision of training at a distance is not a subject of analysis in this book, and the work of Schreiber and Berge (1998) in this area has already been mentioned. It remains, however, to be said that there is no reason why corporate providers, having provided successfully for their in-house staff training, may not, some day, seek a wider market and enter into the provision of distance training, whether electronically or not, to the general public.

Models of accreditation have already been provided by Microsoft, and the Microsoft training certification has become a new benchmark for employment in the computer industry. Should this eventuate, it will once again increase the richness and complexity of offerings of courses at a distance to the public.

6 Training on the World Wide Web

Research carried out in 1998 in the context of the European Commission CISEAR project showed that this area of provision, which started with the first virtual universities in 1995, had already reached maturity.

A series of 80 interviews conducted with global leaders in the field of web-based training, showed that the problems of teaching on the web had already been addressed and students enrolled and taught successfully.

It seems unnecessary, however, to create a new sector of analysis for provision of distance education electronically on the World Wide Web, and it seems better to posit that there are seamless interfaces between non-electronic and electronic distance training.

7 A global model

Many have proposed, and some have feared, the introduction of a global model of distance training, in which the culture of the providing country would be distributed worldwide, either by electronic distance education courses, or by their non-electronic equivalent.

This is only a problem to those who do not know distance systems. Distance systems have for over a hundred years taught students all over the world, frequently with great success.

6   Case studies

Distance training may well be the 'flavour of the month' or have 'gone to the top of the agenda' (Daniel 1999) but it remains relatively unknown. Few understand the daily workings of an open university or a distance training college; the four institutional models identified in this study have not been presented before in the literature; the day-to-day constraints of teaching at a distance are still little understood:

- turn-around of assignments
- certification at a distance
- the shelf-life of courses
- choice of technologies for the home-based student
- cost-effective course production
- choice of technologies that will remain with the same protocol for the shelf-life of courses
- tutor-marked assignments (TMAs) and computer-marked assignments (CMAs)
- the industrialisation of the education process.

To address these concerns a series of case studies is presented. Four institutions representing the four models of this study are chosen from European countries, with the understanding that, *mutatis mutandis*, they are to be found internationally.

These case studies present a cross-section of the EU's institutions, which are at the cutting edge of the current industrialisation of vocational education and training, and the privatisation of institutional learning in Europe. They mirror provision at a distance elsewhere with the proviso that the privatisation of institutional learning is greatly attenuated in group-based distance provision found in the US and elsewhere.

These 16 case studies show the diversity of distance training provision. Even within the institutional groupings there is striking divergence:

- from the large well-established open universities to the new open university foundations in the last few years
- a plethora of strategies for the teaching of courses at a distance from ordinary universities

- in the national characteristics of the government distance training polytechnics
- in the range of proprietary structures, from institutions with six-figure enrolments, to colleges with a few hundred.

The institutions studied represent twelve of the member states of the EU and teach in Spanish, English, Greek, Danish, Catalan, Finnish, Italian, Swedish, French, Dutch, German and Flemish.

For the purposes of analysis each of the case studies follows the same pattern:

1 Title
2 Address
3 Telephone
4 Category
5 Language of provision
6 Official status as a training provider
7 Structure and history
8 Training provision – courses
9 Training provision – certification
10 Training provision – enrolment statistics
11 Course development
12 Student support services
13 Employment provided
14 Plans
15 Web page(s).

These categories are built up from the analysis of the two characteristic subsystems of distance institutions:

- course development subsystem
- student support subsystem

presented in the book *Foundations of Distance Education* (Keegan 1996).

Miller and Rice (1967), in their *Systems of Organisation. The Control of Task and Sentient Boundaries*, showed how organisations can be characterised by their essential operating activities and the importance of analysing task boundaries and sentient (personal) boundaries in administration. In Miller and Rice's terms it is important to identify the 'operating activities' that characterise the enterprise. The operating activities are those that directly contribute to the import/conversion/ export processes which define the nature of the enterprise and differentiate it from other enterprises.

Miller and Rice's theory of system organisation was applied to the organisation of distance education systems by Kaye and Rumble (1981). They had little difficulty in identifying two characteristic operating subsystems, 'course development' and 'student activities', and the task boundaries that separate these activities from other activities within the organisation.

Foundations of Distance Education developed this analysis and showed that the course development subsystem comprises the planning, designing, crystallising, and recording of the teaching, together with the proposed methodologies and structures for presenting the teaching in mechanical or electronic form at a future date. The student support subsystem comprises the activities designed by the institution to focus on the student's home (or institutional or work centre near the student's home) that will provide a private and individualised presentation of the pre-recorded course content, together with the simulation of teacher and peer-group clarification that normally accompanies the presentation of courses in oral, group-based, educational provision.

Distance training enterprises have clusters of task and sentient boundaries which focus on the process of 'course development' and others which focus on the process of' 'support services for students studying at a distance' in a way which cannot be found in other educational institutions. These two characteristic operating sub-systems differentiate them from other forms of educational administration.

The case studies show the contrasting solutions to the challenge of developing systems for students studying at a distance shown in the four models into which the study is divided, and striking national differences within the four models.

Government Distance Training Institutions

1   *Title*:   Centre National d'Enseignement à Distance (CNED).
2   *Address*:   F 86960 Futuroscope, Téléport 2, Boulevard 1, BP 300 and Grenoble, Lille, Lyon, Rennes, Rouen, Toulouse and Vanves (Paris), France.
3   *Telephone*:   00335 49493400.
4   *Category*:   Government distance training institution.
5   *Language of provision*:   French.
6   *Official status as a training provider*:   The CNED is a public administrative establishment of the French Ministry of Education.
7   *Structure and history*:   Founded in 1939, the CNED has its administrative centre at Poitiers-Futuroscope, and eight teaching institutions, each responsible for a national range of programmes.
8   *Training provision – Courses*:   The CNED syllabus lists 3,300 courses at all levels: primary, secondary, technical, vocational, continuing education, university, and postgraduate.
9   *Training provision – Certification*:   All programmes are certified by the Ministry of Education with university degrees being offered by 47 French universities in partnership with the CNED.
10   *Training provision – Enrolment statistics*:   405,000. 200,000 of these are at higher education level. 36,000 are overseas in 207 countries in 2000.
11   *Course development*:   Courses are, in general, developed and maintained by the full-time staff of the CNED.
12   *Student support services*:   Students are, in general, supported by the full-time staff of the CNED. A wide range of services is available and these are usually optional.

13 *Employment provided*: 7,369 staff in 2000.

14 *Plans*: From 2000 onwards the CNED is planning to maintain its vast enrolment, carefully introducing electronic course materials, and internationalising its role.

15 *Web pages*: www.cned.fr

            www.campus-electronic.tm.fr

---

1 *Title*: Centro para la Inovación y Desarrollo de la Educación a Distancia (CIDEAD).

2 *Address*: Argumosa 43, Pabellón 6, 28012, Madrid, Spain.

3 *Telephone*: 00341 527 1546.

4 *Category*: Government Distance Training Institution.

5 *Language of provision*: Spanish.

6 *Official status as a training provider*: The CIDEAD is an institution of the Ministry of Education and Science.

7 *Structure and history*: The CIDEAD was created in 1992 from similar structures going back to 1968.

8 *Training provision – Courses*: Primary education; basic adult training; secondary education; university entry courses; languages; professional updating.

9 *Training provision – Certification*: Courses are certified by the Ministry of Education and Science.

10 *Training provision – enrolment statistics*: 110,000.

11 *Course development*: Courses are developed by consultants and then designed and evaluated by CIDEAD staff.

12 *Student support services*: Student support services are supplied by the CIDEAD which employs 2,000 tutors for this purpose.

13 *Employment provided*: Full-time staff plus 2,000 tutors.

14 *Plans*: The CIDEAD plans to maintain its position as the provider of distance training for children and adults at further education level throughout Spain, in co-operation with the regions.

15 *Web page*: http://www.cidead.es

---

1 *Title*: Bestuur Afstandsonderwijs.

2 *Address*: Konigsstraat 67, 6th floor, 1000 Brussels, Belgium.

3 *Telephone*: 003222114429.

4 *Category*: Government distance training institution.

5 *Language of provision*: Flemish.

6 *Official status as a training provider*: The Bestuur Afstandsonderwijs is a college of the Ministry of the Flemish community, administered by the Education Department, within its Life-Long Training administration.

7 *Structure and history*: The college was founded in 1959 and formed part of a joint French/Flemish distance education provision until 1968.

8   *Training provision – Courses*: There are six groupings of courses:

- languages
- mathematics
- computing and information technology
- economics and administration
- sciences
- technical subjects.

A total of 70 courses is available.

9   *Training provision – Certification*:   The courses are at further education level and many remain within the Bestuur's original mandate of preparing adults for the competitive entry examinations into government employment. Many of the other courses lead to the equivalent of GCSE and 'A' level examinations for adults, or to adult matriculation.

10   *Training provision – enrolment statistics*:   25,000.

11   *Course development*:   Courses are developed, in the main, by the part-time staff of the Bestuur. When the new or revised courses are completed they are sent to the full-time staff for editing, layout, reproduction and printing.

12   *Student support services*:   The student support services are provided by the correction of assignments by the 216 part-time staff who do not communicate with the students but with the full-time staff at the Bestuur who, if necessary, contact the students.

13   *Employment provided*:   23 full-time staff and 216 tutors.

14   *Plans*:   The Bestuur is developing a more user-friendly, more sensitive to students, more upmarket and financially-independent status. New initiatives are a comprehensive computerisation of the administrative systems and courses on the internet.

15   *Web page*:   n/a

---

1   *Title*: Service de l'Enseignement à Distance de la Communauté Française de Belgique.

2   *Address*:   rue Royale 204, Brussels, Belgium.

3   *Telephone*:   00322 2077521.

4   *Category*:   Government distance training institution.

5   *Language of provision*:   French.

6   *Official status as a training provider*:   The service is a college of the Ministry of Education of the French-speaking community in Belgium.

7   *Structure and history*:   The institution was founded in 1959 and until 1968 formed part of a joint French/Flemish distance education provision.

8   *Training provision – Courses*:   Six types of courses are available: adult matriculation, professional preparation for administrative examinations, foreign languages, lifelong learning, courses for Belgian children over-

seas, and courses for hospitalised or disturbed children. 150 courses are provided

9 *Training provision – Certification*: Courses are prepared for study towards the matriculation examinations, for public service examinations regulated by the state, or by the regions, or by the French community, or by provinces, councils and other public bodies, and for professional accreditation bodies.

10 *Training provision – enrolment statistics*: 13,500.

11 *Course development*: Courses are written by the tutors and edited by the staff of the institution who prepare the courses for printing, recording, or the preparation of floppy disks.

12 *Student support services*: Assignments are corrected by the tutors who work at home and whose work is administered by the full-time staff of the college.

13 *Employment provided*: 50 full-time staff and 400 part-time tutors.

14 *Plans*: Plans include putting courses on the internet, and the development of new courses in English and Dutch.

15 *Web page*: n/a.

Proprietary Distance Training Institutions

1 *Title*: Leidse Onderwijsinstellingen.

2 *Address*: Leidsedreef 2, 2352 BA Leiderdorp, Netherlands.

3 *Telephone*: 0033171 – 5451911.

4 *Category*: Proprietary Distance Training Institution.

5 *Language of provision*: Dutch.

6 *Official status as a training provider*: LOI is a training company founded in 1923 and registered in the Netherlands. It also contains a university-level foundation called the LOI Polytechnic, founded in 1996.

7 *Structure and history*: LOI was founded in 1923 as a training company and in 1996 developed a higher education level division.

8 *Training provision – Courses*: LOI offers over 350 courses from basic adult education to polytechnic degrees with courses in subjects ranging from administration, social hygiene, management, tourism, publishing, marketing, 23 languages, journalism, secretarial studies, adult matriculation, technology, para-medical studies, psychology, fitness, house and garden, culture, music, photography and accountancy. The university level programmes are in administration, management, law, marketing, computing, translation and informatics.

9 *Training provision – Certification*: 75 per cent of the courses are for professional qualifications, 15 per cent in languages, and 10 per cent for leisure interest.

10 *Training provision – enrolment statistics*: 110,000: 100,000 in its distance training programmes and 10,000 in its university level programmes.

11 *Course development*: Courses are developed by leading experts in their field, edited at LOI and published in book form or on CD-Roms, video cassettes and floppy disks.

12 *Student support services*: LOI aims to prepare students for their examinations and prepare them to sit successfully for these examinations.

13 *Employment provided*: 1,800.

14 *Plans*: LOI plans to maintain its offering both at higher and further education levels at a distance, and to respond to government requests for a private provider to fill gaps when training shortages occur.

15 *Web page*: http://www.loi.nl

---

1 *Title*: Danmarks Kursuscenter.

2 *Address*: Vibenshus, Lyngbyvej 11/1, 2100, Copenhagen, Denmark.

3 *Telephone*: 004539166700.

4 *Category*: Proprietary distance training institution.

5 *Language of provision*: Danish.

6 *Official status as a training provider*: As a training provider Danmarks Kursuscenter is a privately-owned training institution, controlled by the Danish Ministry of Education, which approves all courses, all the teaching staff and the business administration. All new courses have to be approved by the ministry before they are offered to the public.

7 *Structure and history*: Danmarks Kursuscenter was founded in 1916. The present company is the result of a merger in 1988 between the original foundation and the Merchant Navy Education Centre.

8 *Training provision – Courses*: The institution offers courses for seafarers in the Dutch/Danish Merchant Navy, in addition to personnel in the offshore sectors and leisure-time yachtsmen. These lead to vocational education for seafarers qualifications. In addition the institute offers courses in Danish, English, mathematics, physics and other basic vocational education courses.

9 *Training provision – Certification*: The Danish distance training colleges are not authorised by the Ministry of Education to arrange examinations. 70 per cent of the students, nevertheless, sit for a public examination, which leads to an official qualification recognised by the state.

10 *Training provision – enrolment statistics*: 5,000.

11 *Course development*: Courses are developed by contracted experts and edited and produced by the institution.

12 *Student support services*: Assignments are marked and support services provided by contracted specialists in the course material.

13 *Employment provided*: n/a.

14 *Plans*: The Danmarks Kursuscenter is in the process of developing a polytechnic university at a distance, which will give it a foothold in the higher education market.

15 *Web page*: http://www.dakuce.dk

1 *Title*: Kilroy's College: Irish Correspondence College.
2 *Address*: Cambridge House, Cambridge Road, Dublin 4, Ireland.
3 *Telephone*: 00353 1 6689562.
4 *Category*: Proprietary distance education institution.
5 *Language of provision*: English.
6 *Official status as a training provider*: Kilroy's College is privately-owned and operates through two sister companies, one at national level and the other at international. Many of the courses are aimed at public examinations for high school graduation and public services examinations.
7 *Structure and history*: The Irish Correspondence College was founded in 1932 and in recent years has developed markets in Australia, South Africa, Canada and the Caribbean.
8 *Training provision – Courses*: Kilroy's College offers a wide range of courses in adult matriculation, child psychology, sports psychology, languages, public services examinations and journalism.
9 *Training provision – Certification*: Many of these courses lead to public examinations for which government certification is provided.
10 *Training provision – enrolment statistics*: 8,000.
11 *Course development*: Courses are developed by recognised subject experts on contract, and edited at the college.
12 *Student support services*: Kilroy's College has an excellent record for conscientious assignment-marking and support for its students studying at a distance.
13 *Employment provided*: 25.
14 *Plans*: The College envisages courses on the World Wide Web and in other areas of information technology and is developing agreements with colleges in the UK, Canada, Australia, the US and the Caribbean to market its courses.
15 *Web page*: In development.

---

1 *Title*: Deutsch Weiterbildungsgesellschaft.
2 *Address*: Ostendstrasse 3, 64319, Pfungstadt, Germany.
3 *Telephone*: 004961578060.
4 *Category*: Proprietary distance training institution.
5 *Language of provision*: German.
6 *Official status as a training provider*: The Deutsche Weiterbildungs-gesellschaft, or the German Continuing Education Institution, is a group of training institutions which resulted from the merging of long-established distance training providers in Germany.
7 *Structure and history*: The group is composed of ILS, founded in Hamburg in 1977, AAA founded in 1976, HFB founded in 1996 as a distance polytechnic. HAF is a higher education distance training structure founded in 1997. SWK of Darmstradt is a large distance training college

with a wide range of courses located in Pfungstadt. FEB was founded in 1990. EKS was founded in 1996.

8 *Training provision – Courses*: The main brochure lists 140 courses in business, languages, management, computing studies and technological studies.

9 *Training provision – Certification*: Each course offering is accompanied by its ZFU authorisation number. This means that the courses have been evaluated and approved by the Statliche Zentralstelle für Fernunterricht in Köln, the German government authorisation body.

10 *Training provision – enrolment statistics*: 60,000.

11 *Course development*: All study materials are developed within the group. Authors are contracted to develop material and then the relative institutions edit and produce the materials.

12 *Student support services*: The group states that service to students is their business and that all levels of communication technologies are made available to students, including mail, fax, internet, e-mail and telephone.

13 *Employment provided*: 220 full-time positions and 870 contract positions.

14 *Plans*: The development of the group's private, distance polytechnic or university will be closely observed as the group attempts to set in place a private open university in Germany.

15 *Web page*: http://www.skd.de

Open Universities

1 *Title*: Elliniko Anikto Panepistemio (The Hellenic Open University).

2 *Address*: Papoflese and Ipsitanti Streets, Patros 26222, Greece.

3 *Telephone*: 003061 311048.

4 *Category*: Distance teaching university.

5 *Language of provision*: Greek.

6 *Official status as a training provider*: The Hellenic Open University is a university created by the Greek parliament with the same status as other universities in Greece.

7 *Structure and history*: The bill establishing the Hellenic Open University passed through the Greek parliament on 3 December 1997 and it was gazetted as a university a few days later. It is a national public university. Students were first enrolled on 3 March 1998.

8 *Training provision – Courses*: The Hellenic Open University started with postgraduate certificates in open and distance learning, and English as a second language. These were followed by a full range of graduate and postgraduate courses in the School of Human Studies, the School of Social Sciences, the School of Sciences and Technology, and the School of Applied Arts.

9 *Training provision – Certification*: The university has five types of degrees:

- Certificate of Graduate Education
- First Graduate Degree
- Certificate of Postgraduate Education
- Postgraduate Degree (Masters)
- Doctorate.

All of these are offered at a distance.

10 *Training provision – enrolment statistics*:   Over 20,000 applications were received for the 5,300 places in the first full intake in 1999.
11 *Course development*:   The HOU has formed groups of academics and professionals in different disciplines in order to produce the course material. Courses are also purchased, where available, from existing universities and, as the university develops, the full-time staff of the faculties will take control of course production.
12 *Student support services*:   In each course there are tutorials, at which students have to be present, plus an introductory meeting, telephone communication, written assignments and a final examination.
13 *Employment provided*:   According to the bill granting the university's charter there will be two full-time academics for each module at the university and an additional number of part-time academic staff.
14 *Plans*:   The university plans for schools in Human Studies, Social Studies, Applied Arts, and Science and Technology. These faculties will be assisted by the Laboratory of Educational Materials and the Methodology and Evaluation Unit. The goal is to have the new Open University fully established with 40,000 students enrolled by the year 2002.
15 *Web page*:   www.eap.gr

---

1 *Title*:   Universidad Nacional de Educación a Distancia (UNED).
2 *Address*:   Bravo Murillo 38, 28015 Madrid, Spain.
3 *Telephone*:   003491 3986502.
4 *Category*:   Distance teaching university.
5 *Language of provision*:   Spanish.
6 *Official status as a training provider*:   The UNED was brought into being by decree on 18 August 1972 and has the same official status as all other universities in Spain.
7 *Structure and history*:   The UNED was planned in the 1960s, created in 1972 and has 58 centres, both in Spain and internationally.
8 *Training provision – Courses*:   UNED has a full range of university degrees, with particular emphasis on the faculty of law which has 30 per cent of the students, followed by business administration and psychology.
9 *Training provision – Certification*:   The courses offered by UNED are primarily university level degrees. Degrees are identical to those offered by the other universities, have the same rights and privileges attached,

and carry the appropriate number of credits for evaluation by other institutions. There is a complete postgraduate and doctoral programme at a distance as well.

10   *Training provision – enrolment statistics*:   170,433
11   *Course development*:   Teaching teams are an important part of the structure of UNED and are an important co-ordination tool. Each team prepares the material for its own subjects and selects the method by which the subject will be taught, within the structure of university committees.
12   *Student support services*:   UNED runs a large number of study centres in Spain and elsewhere. Each student must be officially registered at a study centre and must also enrol there. Students attend their tutorials at the centre. They also purchase the necessary teaching units required to participate in the courses, and sit their examinations at the appropriate centre.
13   *Employment provided*:   1,909. This figure breaks down to 869 full-time and 114 part-time academic staff, in addition to 926 administrative and technical staff.
14   *Plans*:   UNED plans to remain a leading open university in Spain with a new development of courses on the World Wide Web.
15   *Web page*:   www.uned.es

---

1   *Title*:   Universitat Oberta de Catalunya.
2   *Address*:   www.uoc.es
3   *Telephone*:   00343 2532300.
4   *Category*:   Distance teaching university.
5   *Language of provision*:   Catalán.
6   *Official status as a training provider*:   The constitutional structure of Spain consists of the central government plus 17 autonomous regions one of which is Catalonia. These autonomous regions may undertake educational provision, or the Central Ministry of Education may exercise this power. The autonomous region of Catalonia founded a distance training university. It has a particular focus on the Catalán language.
7   *Structure and history*:   The UOC was created early in 1995 and quickly became a virtual university based on structures provided by the council, the Chamber of Commerce of Catalonia, the Catalán Savings Bank Federation, the Catalán television, the Catalán radio and the government of the autonomous region of Catalonia.
8   *Training provision – Courses*:   The OUC offers undergraduate and graduate courses. The intention is also to run doctorate and postgraduate programmes.
9   *Training provision – Certification*:   All awards offered are officially recognised by the Ministry of Education and Culture.
10   *Training provision – enrolment statistics*:   12,000 students with 8,000 new enrolments per year.

11 *Course development*: The university develops multimedia modules, multimedia support materials, reference works, simulations or experiments and case studies. The main media used are e-mail, computer conferencing, printed materials, electronic editions of materials, video and television via Catalán public broadcasting.

12 *Student support services*: OUC students are required to have a personal computer, printer, modem, television, cassette player and video cassette player and it is possible to use the equipment provided at the centres throughout Catalonia. This would, however, mean losing many of the advantages of having the virtual campus at one's disposal, at home, 24 hours a day.

13 *Employment provided*: 134 full-time staff; 150 part-time academic staff.

14 *Plans*: The Open University of Catalonia plans to develop itself as Europe's first government virtual university and to widen its course base to include postgraduate level qualifications.

15 *Web page*: www.uoc.es

---

1 *Title*: The Open University of the United Kingdom (OUUK).

2 *Address*: Walton Hall, Milton Keynes, UK.

3 *Telephone*: 0044 1908 274066.

4 *Category*: Distance teaching university.

5 *Language of provision*: English.

6 *Official status as a training provider*: The Open University was created by Royal Charter in 1969 and enrolled its first students in 1971. Its charter enables it to award degrees on the same basis as other universities in the UK.

7 *Structure and history*: The Open University was created in 1969 and established as an independent and autonomous institution authorised to confer its own degrees and undertake professional training. It has regional offices all over the UK and organises a range of study centres for students' tutorial activities and, in the summer, uses other British residential universities for its summer schools.

8 *Training provision – Courses*: The OU brochure, *Studying with the Open University*, lists the courses in the following groupings:

- Social Science
- Health and Social Welfare
- Community Education
- Mathematics and Computing
- Postgraduate Computing and Manufacturing

- Technology
- Education
- Science
- Environment
- Management (run by the Open Business School).

9 *Training provision – Certification*: The OU offers certificates and diplomas, BA and BSc degrees, taught higher degrees, postgraduate certificates in education, and doctorates.

10 *Training provision – enrolment statistics*:   The latest published statistics give 112,471 undergraduates, 27,843 taught higher degrees, 833 research part-time degrees and 594 research full-time degrees. In addition there are 15,105 in overseas schemes, 7,174 validated students from other colleges and 1,269 non-credit enrolments. Training packages: 44,163.

11 *Course development*:   Courses are developed by course teams. A first-year foundation course can have as many as 20 full-time Open University or BBC staff assigned to it, plus consultants, instructional designers and media experts. The course team designs a total learning package comprising printed materials, home experiment kits, BBC television programmes, audio and video cassettes, teaching strategies, and induction and training programmes for those who will tutor and counsel students enrolled in the course in the years to come.

12 *Student support services*:   The OUUK provides:

- a tutor-counsellor who follows the student's progress throughout his/her university career
- a tutor for consultation on an individual course
- 13 regional offices, providing a decentralised focus for the administration of tuition, counselling and student support systems
- a study centre within easy travelling distance where the student can meet others and use facilities.

In addition OUUK students sent 70,000,000 e-mails in 1999 and these were read an average of 10 times each, creating a vast electronic discussion and analysis structure for academic interaction.

13 *Employment provided*:   10,809 staff. This comprises 918 academics, 1,046 academic-related, 1,730 administrative, 198 BBC staff and 6,917 part-time lecturers.

14 *Plans*:   New initiatives include law and languages, computing technologies and the knowledge media, and the development of courses for the World Wide Web.

15 *Web page*:   http://www.open.ac.uk

Distance Education Courses from a University

1 *Title*: Heriot-Watt University.
2 *Address*: Riccarton, Edinburgh, EHI4 4AS, Scotland.
3 *Telephone*: 0044131 4495111.
4 *Category*: Distance education provision from a university.
5 *Language of provision*: English.
6 *Official status as a training provider*: The MBA at a distance from the Edinburgh Business School has the same standing as any other higher degree offered by Heriot-Watt University.
7 *Structure and history*: The Edinburgh Business School is the business faculty of Heriot-Watt University. The distance education provision of the Master of Business Administration commenced in October 1990.

8 *Training provision – Courses*: The Master of Business Administration is a degree at master's level.

9 *Training provision – Certification*: Same status as any other higher degree from Heriot-Watt University.

10 *Training provision – enrolment statistics*: 15,000.

11 *Course development*: The texts for the Heriot-Watt MBA are specially written with the distance learner in mind. Most modules contain learning objectives that clearly state the key points expected to be learned in each section, and one or more sample examinations with model solutions. The modules are self-contained texts. All features of the Heriot-Watt MBA are designed for practical business application.

12 *Student support services*: The Heriot-Watt MBA by distance learning is non-residential. It provides graduation in absentia; is self-paced; provides examinations and courses; a long-term study plan; open access; no need for a bachelor's degree as a prerequisite.

13 *Employment provided*: 50 of the university's 2,400 staff are employed in the distance learning programme.

14 *Plans*: Recent developments include an important web presence and plans to consider an undergraduate business course.

15 *Web page*: www.heriotwatt.ac.uk.

---

1 *Title*: University of Oulu.

2 *Address*: University Oulu, Kiviharjuntic 11, FIN 9022, Finland.

3 *Telephone*: 00 358 85376300.

4 *Category*: Distance education provision from a university.

5 *Language of provision*: Finnish.

6 *Official status as a training provider*: The University of Oulu is a public university of the Finnish government. Its distance education programme is called the Open University activities of its Continuing Education Department. The continuing education market is for professional and government structures in Finland and constitutes a market for paying customers for the university.

7 *Structure and history*: The university was founded in 1958, 1,000 kilometres north of Helsinki. The University of Oulu has five faculties with a total of 12,000 students. The distance education programme, which enrols 2,000 of these students, is called the Open University of the Continuing Education Centre of the university. It has a special mandate for the 800,000 people who live in the sphere of influence of the university, of whom 100,000 live in the town of Oulu.

8 *Training provision – Courses*: Distance education courses are provided in the humanities and education, science and technology and medicine. These courses are open to all.

9 *Training provision – Certification*: Studies in the distance education courses are open to all, and students are fully credited for their courses at

the University of Oulu. However, graduation for a degree is possible only if the student is accepted by the university.

10 *Training provision – enrolment statistics*: 2,000.

11 *Course development*: Courses are developed to match customer needs, and also to follow the directions of development in videoconferencing and on the internet, and especially in information and communication technologies.

12 *Student support services*: The distance education programme is part of the University of Oulu Centre for Continuing Education's responsibility for the 800,000 who live in the northern half of Finland.

13 *Employment provided*: 2,500. Seven are employed in the Continuing Education Centre, with about 200 part-time staff available from the university.

14 *Plans*: The University of Oulu has an interest in new learning environments. Face-to-face teaching is still the most typical mode of studying but there is a development of new technology and new study models. The Continuing Education Centre will continue the development of new learning structures in co-operation with the university Faculty of Education, where research work is done on distance learning.

15 *Web page*: www.oulu.fi

---

1 *Title*: Linköping University.

2 *Address*: Linköping University, Linköping, Sweden.

3 *Telephone*: 004613281000.

4 *Category*: Distance education provision from a university.

5 *Language of provision*: Swedish.

6 *Official status as a training provider*: The Linköping University follows the Swedish concept of providing distance education courses from conventional universities. All faculties are involved. The university currently offers some 50 separate distance taught courses and a few additional study programmes.

7 *Structure and history*: The University of Linköping was first founded as an independent college and then became a university in 1975 with three faculties:

- The Institute of Technology
- The Faculty of Arts and Sciences
- The Faculty of Health and Sciences.

Linköping University is a member of the Swedish consortium for distance education, which includes the Universities of Lund, Umeå, Uppsala, the Royal Institute of Technology and the University of Vaxjo.

8 *Training provision – Courses*: All the faculties of Linköping offer distance education courses. Often the courses consist of face-to-face lectures with periods of self study in between, without many guiding

materials. At Linköping distance education has been an integrated part of undergraduate education since the distance education courses started in the early 1970s.

9 *Training provision – Certification*: All courses are certified by the university.

10 *Training provision – enrolment statistics*: 2,000.

11 *Course development*: The principal teaching medium is printed material such as study guides, written assignments, reading instruction, study or review questions. Other media include television, videoconferencing, video and audio cassettes, the use of computers and e-mail, with local study centres for tutorial support.

12 *Student support services*: Many distance courses require meetings, lectures, tutoring and laboratory sessions.

13 *Employment provided*: n/a

14 *Plans*: Linköping University is the only university in Sweden that offers distance education by means of the terrestrial television broadcasting network, U-LINK. It plans to continue this development and developments on the World Wide Web and to maintain the Swedish concept of providing distance education courses from conventional universities.

15 *Web page*: www.liu.se.

---

1 *Title*: Università degli Studi di Roma III.

2 *Address*: Department of Education, Via del Castro Pretorio 20, 00185 Rome, Italy.

3 *Telephone*: 0039 06 4957805.

4 *Category*: Distance education provision from a university.

5 *Language of provision*: Italian.

6 *Official status as a training provider*: The University of Rome III is the provider. The distance education programme is run by the Department of Educational Sciences of the Faculty of Education. Italian university legislation, especially the DPR 162 of 10 March 1982, authorises the institution of postgraduate degrees in specialised professional fields.

7 *Structure and history*: In 1986, the university received numerous requests from schools and other organisations that teachers be upgraded and this led to the decision to create the first postgraduate course at a distance in the methods of educational evaluation. In subsequent years, due to the success of the initiative, other courses were added to this first offering. The target for these courses is teachers in schools or new university graduates who envisage entering the teaching profession.

8 *Training provision – Courses*: Four courses are offered:

• Methods of Educational Evaluation
• General Didactics for Museums
• Didactical Principles
• Educational Technology.

9   *Training provision – Certification*:   All courses are certified by the university.

10   *Training provision – enrolment statistics*:   2,360.

11   *Course development*:   Courses consist of modules, each of which comprises a printed volume, including tests and examinations specially developed for the distance education students. The didactic activities for the distance education courses form part of the official workload of the professors of the university, exactly as their didactic responsibilities for face-to-face students. For certain specific themes within the distance education provision, experts from outside the department are brought in.

12   *Student support services*:   The didactic structure of the programme has the goal of providing procedures for realising two-way communication and focusing on the individualisation of the learning process. The department employs a system of computer correction. This system allows the correction of examinations and the automatic production of individualised compensatory reports. In addition there are two meetings which take place during the course of the year, which are obligatory.

13   *Employment provided*:   Most of the people involved in the distance education programme work as either lecturers or in administration at the university and give part of their time to the administration and the didactics of the distance education programme. 79 people are involved in this way.

14   *Plans*:   The university plans to develop further distance education courses, especially on the internet, through other faculties, especially the faculty of Electronic Engineering

15   *Web page*:   www.uniroma3.it/LPS/

7 Can academic excellence be achieved at a distance?

Achieving excellence

There is little value in putting forward distance training as an important sector of training in the new millennium if students cannot achieve excellence at a distance.

As a harbinger of what is to come, excellence should already have been achieved. As a form of provision in the future, excellence should be able to be guaranteed. If academic excellence at a distance cannot be achieved in training certificates, college diplomas and university degrees at a distance, whether electronic or not, then little credence can be accorded to this form of provision.

Research and practice on the achievement of excellence are examined in this chapter.

Research

Dubin and Taveggia

In 1968 Dubin and Taveggia from the University of Oregon published *The Teaching-Learning Paradox: A Comparative Analysis of College Teaching Methods*.

This research provided the foundations for the achievement of academic excellence in distance education programmes, whether electronic or not.

Dubin and Taveggia demonstrated that no particular method of college instruction is measurably to be preferred over another, when evaluated by student examination performances. Methods of college instruction analysed included lectures, seminars, instructional television, correspondence courses, or any combination of these, and their findings can confidently be applied to the electronic distance education courses of today.

They examined data on 7,000,000 adult or near-adult students studying at two- and four-year American higher education institutions, or universities, to find the relations between the various methods of instruction and the outcomes produced, when measured by final examinations on the courses.

Their conclusions were decisive: the method of instruction chosen did not affect student performance. They also concluded that replication of their work would not produce conclusions different from theirs.

One can agree with them. So vast was their database and their meta-analyses that there seems to be little value in repeating their work. Their conclusions have not been challenged since they were published 30 years ago.

In spite of its claims, the work of the University of Oregon researchers has not been widely analysed in the distance training literature. For this reason it is presented here in detail:

Dubin and Taveggia set out the research agenda thus:

> Analytically we want to measure the utility of one college teaching method over another. We believe that teaching is a technology, the content of which can be rationally ordered by some distinctive model of the teaching process. (1968:2)

They then set out the two technologies that set the extremes of practice that they wished to investigate:

> The lecture method assumes the superior knowledge of the lecturer and therefore places in his hands the selection of subject matter to be covered, the depth of coverage to be employed, the balance between content and illustration, the length of the lecture period, and the frequency of the lectures in a given period of time.
>
> By way of contrast, self-study (this usually means a reading list and a limited period of time to complete the reading) limits the superiority of the instructor to a knowledge of the relevant bibliography of his field. Beyond that it is assumed that the student learns through interaction with the printed materials. The book rather than the instructor becomes the teacher. (1968:2)

They gave the research context of their work as:

> It seems reasonable to assume that given such distinctive teaching technologies as lecture, on the one hand, and self-study on the other hand, there should be measurable differences in outcomes of these two methods. It is the very reasonableness of such an expectation that leads to the conclusion that there will, indeed, be measurable differences between any two contrasting teaching methods. (1968:10)

Dubin and Taveggia produced an educational 'law': the achievement of academic excellence does not depend on the method of instruction whether face-to-face or at a distance or on the web. The variables for student success or failure lie elsewhere.

Schramm

A decade later confirmation for Dubin and Taveggia's findings was provided by the publication of Schramm's (1977) *Big Media, Little Media*.

Schramm worked at the East/West Centre in Hawaii, mainly in the comparison of lectures with textbooks, lectures with motion pictures, pictures with text or instructional (educational) television, or teaching machines, or computerised instruction.

He concluded that:

- No single medium is likely to have properties that make it best for all purposes.
- Most instructional functions can be performed by most media.
- Big media have no inherent advantages over little media.
- Expensive media have no pedagogical advantages over cheaper media.

Thus the technique used is not *per se* a major element in the success or failure of a course of instruction. Bigger and more expensive media do not *per se* contribute to successful learning any more than less expensive media.

Clark

Further evidence was provided by Clark from the University of Southern California in the early 1980s.

He claimed that media do not influence learning under any conditions and that 'media are mere vehicles that deliver instruction but do not influence student achievement any more than the truck that delivers our groceries causes changes in our nutrition'.

According to Clark (1983:445–59) 50 years of research have shown that there are no learning benefits to be gained from employing different media in instruction, regardless of their obviously attractive features or advertised superiority.

Clark words his conclusions thus:

> One might reasonably wonder why media are still advocated for their ability to increase learning when research shows clearly that such benefits are not forthcoming. Of course such conclusions are disseminated slowly and must compete with the advertising budgets of the multimillion-dollar industry, which has a vested interest in selling their machines for instruction. An equal contributor to this disparity between research and practice is the high expectation we have for technology of all kinds. (1983:456)

Clark focused on the high expectation that people have from technology of all kinds, an expectation even higher today. Machine-based technologies, he says, have revolutionised industry and people have had understandable hopes that machine-based technologies would also benefit education.

Russell

At http://cuda.teleeducation.nb.ca/nosignificantdifference/ (visited 1/12/99) one gets the 'No Significant Difference Phenomenon' website on a TeleEducation, New Brunswick, server.

This is a compilation of 355 research reports, analyses and papers compiled by Thomas L. Russell, until recently Director of the Office of Instructional Telecommunications of North Carolina State University, on the theme that there is no significant difference between face-to-face teaching and distance education. See Figure 7.1.

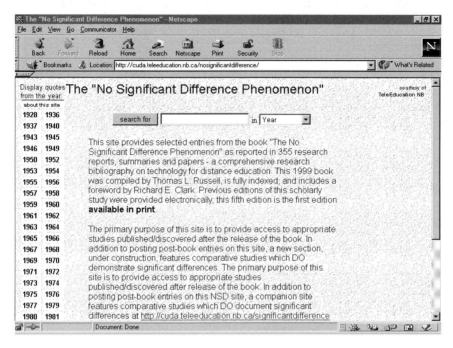

Figure 7.1 Russell's The 'No Significant Difference Phenomenon'

This compilation has been built up on the web for a number of years as Russell collected and summarised on his site, books, articles and statistical reports dealing with the theme.

It is a comprehensive archive of references to all major studies of the evaluation of academic achievement using any instructional methodology. The site has recently been revised and published in book form with a foreword by Clark.

Conclusion

For over 50 years studies have been conducted on students taught in face-to-face classes, training centres, seminars and lectures and on those taught at a distance.

The almost invariable result of these studies is that there is no significant difference between distance education and on-campus provision.

The variables of successful learning, of quality of learning, of the retention of learning, of the transfer of learning to the workplace, lie elsewhere.

Dubin and Taveggia, Schramm, Clark, Russell and others have shown that academic excellence can be achieved by distance education, whether in non-electronic systems or in virtual systems on the web.

This is excellent news for those working in the provision of training at a distance, or on the web, or using some other non-traditional methodology: one does not have to be rich to learn; one does not have to enrol in an expensive system, or use expensive technologies to learn; certificates, diplomas and degrees won at a distance can be as good as those won in training centres or universities; academic excellence is achievable at a distance.

Practice

It is best, however, to ask what happens in fact, in practice. Analysis is provided from the University of New England at Armidale in Australia, the CNED in France and the OUUK at Milton Keynes.

University of New England (UNE)

One of the earlier attempts seriously to address the question of parity of achievement between distance education students and students attending universities, was undertaken in 1979 by K. Smith, the then Director of External Studies at UNE. In the silver jubilee report on external studies at his university, Smith (1979) compared data on off-campus and on-campus students over a period of 25 years, from 1954 to 1979.

What made the study significant was that Smith's university followed what was sometimes known as the 'Australian integrated mode' form of provision. This meant that professors and lecturers at the university had equal responsibility for teaching off-campus and on-campus students and, other things being equal, contractual responsibility for equal groupings of external and on-campus students. It also meant that the external students had the same curricula, the same textbooks, the same tutors, the same assignments, the same examinations and the same evaluators as those who were in residence at the university.

Many of the on-campus students were recent school-leavers with excellent results in their HSCs (Higher School Certificates); some of the external students were farmers on their properties who had not studied since primary school.

Smith was able to show, that, not only was there no significant difference between the external and on-campus students, but that university medals for academic excellence in particular faculties or departments were won by external students.

Centre National d'Enseignement à Distance (CNED)

At the time of writing the CNED is celebrating its sixtieth anniversary and is by far Europe's largest government training provider, and largest distance training provider, with courses at higher education level, further education level, and a considerable enrolment of children at primary and secondary level as well.

A feature of the French educational system is that certification is characterised by government awards and examinations or competitions at every level from children's schooling to postgraduate university degrees.

This may not be a system that appeals to some commentators from Anglo-Saxon backgrounds but it can work in favour of distance education. Over many years one can analyse the results of the students who studied with the CNED, and the students who went to schools, training centres and universities, and show that parity of achievement can be realised.

Open University of the United Kingdom (OUUK)

The OUUK lives in the highly competitive British higher education market: there are the universities, the Open University, and perhaps 100 of the conventional universities also competing for the distance education market. All of these are funded, at least in part, by taxpayers' monies.

The most recent issue of the *UCAS Guide*, the government listing of higher education institutions issued to school-leavers to assist them in their application for university study, details 199 higher education providers, 24 of which are structures within the University of London.

In the mid-1990s the British government set about measuring the academic excellence of all the universities and publishing its results.

Although some commentators from non-Anglo-Saxon countries look askance at the measurement of academic excellence, it is a system that can work in favour of distance education.

The first published results showed the Open University in the top ten in the UK, along with two tutorial universities (Oxford and Cambridge) and only seven conventional universities, three of which, London School of Economics (LSE), University College London (UCL) and Imperial, are structures within the University of London.

A media presentation of these statistics is given in Figure 7.2.

To reach these rankings the UK government Quality Assurance Agency puts together panels each year to go and look at the quality of teaching in particular disciplines in each university that teaches them.

The teams have to assess the quality of teaching in the discipline in each university on six dimensions:

- Curriculum design, content and organisation;
- Teaching, learning and assessment:
- Student progression and achievement:
- Student support and guidance;
- Learning resources;
- Quality assurance and enhancement.

The university's teaching is rated on a scale of four on each of these six dimensions, so the maximum score a university can get for the teaching of a particular discipline is 24/24.

Premier League (50%+ Excellent)	Division 1 (35–50% Excellent)	Division 2 (20–34% Excellent)	Division 3 (5–20% Excellent)	Division 4 (No Excellents)
Cambridge	Edinburgh	Essex	Sheffield Hallam	Bournemouth
York	Birmingham	Oxford Brookes	East London	Humberside
Oxford	Glasgow	Surrey	Nottingham Trent	Staffordshire
Imperial	Bristol	Sussex	Thames Valley	John Moores
LSE	Leeds	Liverpool	Central Lancaster	Luton
Warwick	Cardiff	Northumbria	London Guildhall	Paisley
UCL	King's London	Aberdeen	Huddersfield	Sunderland
Durham	UMIST	Queen Mary & Westfield	Goldsmiths'	Napier
Sheffield	West of England	Reading	Lampeter	Brighton
Open University	Manchester	Leicester	Portsmouth	Salford
Southampton	East Anglia	Stirling	Central England	Bradford
Nottingham	Bath	Ulster	Birkbeck	Middlesex
Lancaster	Hull	Plymouth	Heriot-Watt	
Bangor	Exeter	Kent	Abertay Dundee	
St Andrews	Queen's Belfast	Dundee	Leeds Metropolitan	
	Strathclyde	Coventry	Manchester Metropolitan	
	Loughborough	Glamorgan	North London	
	Newcastle	City	South Bank	
	Swansea	Greenwich	Teesside	
	Brunei	Keele	Hertfordshire	
	Aberystwyth	Aston	Robert Gordon	
		Anglia	De Montfort	
		Kingston	Westminster	
		Royal Holloway	Derby	
			Glasgow Caledonian	
			Wolverhampton	

Figure 7.2 Media presentation of UK universities' quality leagues

Figure 7.3 shows the official government criteria used for ranking UK universities:

Dimensions of Quality

Higher Education Funding Council for England

1   Curriculum design, content and organisation.

2   Teaching, learning and assessment.

3   Student progression and achievement.

4   Student support and guidance.

5   Learning resources.

6   Quality assurance and enhancement.

(Assessment of a scale of one to four on each dimension)

Figure 7.3 Measurement of academic excellence at universities in the UK

Among the subjects in which the Open University has been rated excellent are Chemistry, Geology, Music, Business, and Engineering. These are all subjects where one would not think that a distance teaching university had a natural advantage.

It follows that over 100 British universities and institutes of higher education have been rated as inferior to the Open University. When one realises that these conventional universities use their full-time professors, readers, senior lecturers and lecturers to teach full-time students who have qualified with outstanding 'A' levels, while the Open University teaches part-time students at a distance, nearly 40 per cent of whom would not have academic qualifications acceptable to face-to-face universities, one can see the extent of the distance university's achievement.

It comes as somewhat of a surprise that up to 100 of these face-to-face universities choose to challenge the Open University in the distance education market, often with small departments staffed by part-time consultants, when their full-time professorial staff have failed to match the academic excellence of the Open University with their ordinary students.

Conclusion

Both from research and practical evidence it seems clear that academic excellence can be achieved by distance systems, whether they teach by 'traditional' distance education or on the web.

In 1993 a questionnaire was devised for the evaluation of students participating in an Irish satellite-based course taught from University College Dublin to a series of regional technical colleges throughout the country (Keegan 1995a).

The satellite delivery model was evaluated from five aspects:

- *Academic excellence*: Could academic excellence be achieved? Was it possible to produce a rigorous university-level teaching and learning system by satellite?
- *Access*: Did students enrol who would otherwise have been unable to do the course?
- *Quality of learning*: Would students be hampered in their learning by the absence of lectures from a physically present lecturer?
- *Results*: Would students be confident of passing? Would they drop out in large numbers? Would their assignment and final examination results be as good as a student who travelled regularly to the university?
- *Status*: After the experience of a satellite university course would they enrol again in satellite-delivered courses?

The effectiveness of satellite provision questionnaire was completed by all students (N = 218) in December 1993, soon after they became familiar with the system.

The questionnaire was designed to provoke precise responses by the use of provocative terminology, not frequently used in educational questionnaires. Students were asked to evaluate 'academic excellence' and not whether the course was successful or not. Students were asked if their studying was 'hampered' because they did not attend face-to-face lectures. Students were asked if their university examination results were 'just as good as if' they had attended lectures at the university. Students were asked if they 'would enrol again' in a satellite-delivered course, and whether they would advise their friends and colleagues to enrol in a satellite-delivered course.

The results are striking, with 86 per cent stating that academic excellence could be achieved by satellite, 82 per cent refusing to accept that their studying was hampered, and 94 per cent stating that they would enrol again in a satellite-delivered course. The results were published with the statistical evidence presented thus:

1   It is possible to achieve academic excellence in a satellite-delivered course.

- *Strongly agree*   23 per cent
- *Agree*   63 per cent
- *Uncertain*   14 per cent
- *Disagree*   0 per cent
- *Strongly disagree* 0 per cent.

2   My enrolment was dependent on the course being offered by satellite at a centre near to me.

- *Strongly agree*   41 per cent
- *Agree*   33 per cent
- *Uncertain*   7 per cent
- *Disagree*   15 per cent
- *Strongly disagree* 3 per cent.

3   My learning from the course was hampered because I did not attend face-to-face lectures.

- *Strongly agree*   1 per cent
- *Agree*   5 per cent
- *Uncertain*   11 per cent
- *Disagree*   66 per cent
- *Strongly disagree*   16 per cent.

4   My examination results will be just as good as if I had studied with face-to-face lectures at the university.

- *Strongly agree*   16 per cent
- *Agree*   56 per cent
- *Uncertain*   23 per cent
- *Disagree*   5 per cent
- *Strongly disagree*   1 per cent.

5   I would enrol again in a satellite-delivered course.

- *Strongly agree*   40 per cent
- *Agree*   54 per cent
- *Uncertain*   6 per cent
- *Disagree*   0 per cent
- *Strongly disagree*   1 per cent.

The same questionnaire with its provocative terminology was used later to evaluate a videoconference programme in which the trainer was in Ireland and the students were in Sweden, using a two-way video, two-way audio videoconferencing system. In the published results of the videoconferencing system ratings of over or near 90 per cent were achieved in the five questions, couched in identical terms to the satellite study (Keegan 1995b).

In 1998 and again in 1999, the same questionnaire was applied to students studying on the World Wide Web, in an Irish multinational web-based training system. The results are published at http://www.nki.no/eeileo/research.html. Again the percentage who claimed academic excellence, increased access, no hampering of study success, excellent examination results, willingness to enrol again, and willingness to advise colleagues and friends to enrol in web-based training, was at or near 90 per cent.

Quality control

The achievement of academic excellence at a distance and the arrival of new stakeholders in the field, both on the World Wide Web and using other media, raise the question of quality control.

The UK government addressed these issues in 1999 with the publication of *Guidelines in the Quality Assurance of Distance Learning* by its Quality Assurance Agency for Higher Education.

This is a detailed presentation which supports the guidelines for evaluation proposed in *Foundations of Distance Education*:

- excellence in course development procedures, especially in the structuring of the content of courses;
- excellence in student support services while the students are studying the course;
- excellence in logistics and administration, for students who may be all over the world;
- excellence in research on the theory and practice of distance education.

The UK government publication gives detailed guidelines on six major areas of distance learning for evaluation and quality control:

- system design
- programme design
- the management of programme delivery
- student development and support
- student communication and representation
- student assessment.

There is an important emphasis in these guidelines on the student support services half of a distance training system, rather than on the development of materials, electronic or otherwise. This balance in favour of the student support services is valid. It is the quality of student learning from the materials which justifies the awarding of nationally- and internationally-recognised degrees and diplomas by representatives of this sector of educational provision to students who may never visit their institutions.

8   The distance training industry market

From private to public

A remarkable shift has occurred in the last 30 years in distance training provision. This shift has seen an increase in government-funded provision of distance training worldwide. Prior to 1970, most of the provision of distance education and training, apart from the government distance training institutions in France, Australia and New Zealand, and a small provision of courses at a distance from certain universities, was proprietary.

This chapter seeks to give a market observatory of the provision of distance training in the EU as a sample of possible trends worldwide. As throughout this book, the focus is on courses that are available to citizens for enrolment at certificate, diploma or degree level.

One can gauge the importance of distance training to a national government by whether or not it has decided to found a national distance education system, like the CNED in France, or a distance teaching university, like the open universities in many countries in the world.

The reason why one can gauge a government's commitment to distance training in this way, and by implication its commitment to the training of working taxpayers and its citizens over 25, is that to provide a distance system a government has to use taxpayers' monies twice. A government uses taxpayers' monies once to provide schools and colleges and universities to which, however, the distance students choose not to or are unable to go. It uses taxpayers' monies the second time to set up institutions like the CNED, or the *Dianda* network, which teach only at a distance, for their citizens who choose not to attend schools or colleges.

Government involvement in distance training

Three of the four sectors of distance training identified in this book deal with government provision: open universities, government distance training institutions, conventional university provision. There is little analysis of the history of government funding of distance training in the literature, so a brief outline is provided here.

In the nineteenth century distance education courses were offered from a number of universities in the US, but this was invariably a private initiative by a lecturer or a department, and did not involve government financing.

The entry of governments into training at a distance can be traced to the year 1909, in which a health inspector, named William Alan Grundy, started correspondence courses for rural health nurses, in outback New South Wales, in Australia. It is claimed that there is a direct line from his work through to the foundation of the New South Wales College of External Studies in the 1960s, to the Open Training and Education Network (OTEN) of the New South Wales government Department of Technical and Further Education today.

In 1910, the University of Queensland, in Australia, was created and immediately started teaching at a distance. This was because it was a university of a state, and not a university of a city, like Oxford or Bologna or Sydney or Melbourne, and because it had the whole state with an electorally-important, and widely-scattered, farming community as its campus.

The following year, in 1911, the labour government of Western Australia, initiated a correspondence programme as well.

From 1914, each Australian state government and the government of New Zealand and each Canadian provincial government, set up a distance education school for the education of isolated, hospitalised and other children unable to attend a local school. The earliest was at Melbourne, in the state of Victoria (1914), followed by Sydney, New South Wales (1916), Perth, Western Australia (1918), Hobart, Tasmania (1919), Adelaide, South Australia (1920), Brisbane, Queensland (1922), Wellington, New Zealand (1922) and the foundations by the Ministries of Education of the Canadian provinces followed. In Australia the short-wave radio Schools of the Air for children in the outback were later added to this provision.

In France in 1939, and again for children, the French Ministry of Education founded the Centre National d'Enseignement par Correspondance (CNEC). In the aftermath of World War II, the state governments of Australia and the government of New Zealand set up government vocational education and training at distance colleges, on a model remarkably similar to the French system. The goal was the speedy training of soldiers demobilised from the forces and the retraining of the workforce after the war. This lead was later followed by the governments of Belgium and Spain.

The period 1950 to 1970 was characterised also by an investment in distance education by the communist governments of the Republics of Central and Eastern Europe and of the People's Republic of China, including both distance education institutions, and distance education departments of conventional universities.

In spite of these early foundations, and the lengthy period of government funding of distance training at various levels and in various parts of the world, it was the foundation, in the 1970s, of a series of distance teaching universities, known today as 'the open universities', which had a major impact on the market and on the quality and quantity of provision. Nations today, which did not found an open university, often encourage provision from all, or a selection of, their existing conventional universities.

Market analysis

For a market analysis, it is clear that society provides itself with privileged places, where the teaching/learning process takes place. These are called schools or colleges or training centres or universities. Citizens who study at a distance choose not to frequent the schools, colleges and universities that society provides, or are unable to do so and choose to study at home or, in some cases, at work. In the group-based systems in the US and elsewhere, they come together at a remote location owned by or hired by, or loaned to, the university or training centre at which the course is being delivered to other groups of students. These students expect to be awarded their certificates and diplomas and even university degrees at home or work.

Society, therefore, in parallel to the provision of schools, colleges and universities, provides distance schools and distance colleges and distance universities, or distance departments of ordinary universities, to teach those who choose to study at home, or at work.

The politico-economic challenge facing national governments in the twenty-first century is whether to invest in conventional schools, training centres, colleges and universities (*conventional education*), or distance schools, colleges and open universities (*distance education*), or virtual schools, colleges and universities (*virtual education*) in which citizens will be taught electronically.

European statistics

The research reported in this book provides a market observatory of how citizens behave in the purchase of distance training courses for vocational purposes at the turn of the millennium. The results are detailed in Figure 8.1.

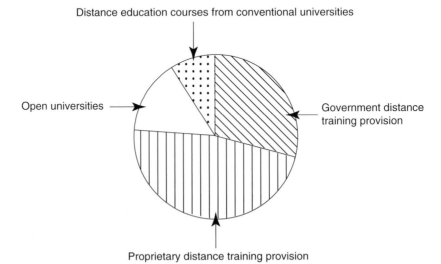

Figure 8.1 Purchase of vocational training at a distance by EU citizens 1999

Over 70 per cent of the enrolment is in further education courses at a distance. Only 30 per cent is at university level. It was never likely that university-level courses could compete with the 450,000 enrolled in the Charkov Beheer, based in the Netherlands, and the 405,000 enrolled in the CNED, which is here regarded as a further education structure.

Spain and France are shown as major providers. This may come as a surprise, as much of the literature is written about Anglo-Saxon systems.

Systems which provide courses aimed at the technologies in citizens' homes still have a large share of the market: there seems, as yet, little correlation between high technology systems and market control.

The focus in the literature and at conferences on state-of-the-art technologies has not had much impact on the market place, although the data for Scandinavia may indicate the start of a trend towards higher technology systems.

Fees paid

In this market observatory the focus is on the annual volume of fees paid by citizens for distance training programmes, to either government or private colleges or universities.

In a market observatory it is important to calculate, not only the annual volume of fees paid for distance training programmes. One must also attempt to estimate the volume of fees paid for enrolments by government agencies from taxpayers' monies.

The volume of fees paid from taxpayers' funds by governments to distance training providers is difficult to quantify. In some instances the fee is part of an annual grant from taxpayers' money to the distance training providers; at times it is in the form of a capitation grant; at times it is in the form of a subsidy to the individual enrolling. Sometimes this is free of income tax consequences, sometimes it is taxable. Sometimes the full cost of the enrolment is provided, sometimes the fee paid is a composite of payment by the citizen enrolling, plus a subsidy from local or central government tax revenues.

The rules accepted here for establishing the market volume are:

*   Fee payment, or fee subsidisation, is only counted once in the fiscal year of the actual enrolment. Thus, many programmes last eighteen months or more, but are only counted once.
*   Fees are counted only in the country from which the course is offered. Thus a student studying a Fernuniversität programme in Vienna is counted in Germany.

To make the procedures more precise, the following additional rules are stipulated:

*   the focus is the number of citizens actually enrolled in distance training in the year in question
*   multiple enrolments are ignored

- the length of the enrolment is ignored
- the number of hours' training per week is ignored
- the level of qualification is ignored
- parity of esteem is accorded to all programmes.

There are other possible bases for calculating the volume of the distance training industry market in an area, but those are for other studies.

To quantify the annually recurring EU market these procedures are followed:

- an average enrolment fee is calculated from the data for each of the 64 cells in the study;
- total fees paid are calculated by multiplying the volume of enrolments in each cell by the average fee for each cell.

A study by Van der Mark (1993) had calculated the average range of fees in the EU at between €100 and €1000. This is a wide range. The real figure probably lies within this range, except for some MBA programmes at a distance which attract considerably higher fees.

The data collected in this study indicate that the average fee paid lies in the region of €350 to €450. As the volume of citizens enrolling, or being enrolled, each year is calculated at over 3,000,000, it follows that the annually recurring market volume is quantified at over one billion euros.

The cost-effectiveness of distance training

One reason for the growth of distance training provision is its cost-effectiveness in comparison to both conventional provision, and to other forms of open, flexible or technology-based provision.

The rules for cost-effectiveness in distance systems were provided by, amongst others, Rumble (1997) of the OUUK. An overview of similar issues was given in *Foundations of Distance Education* (Keegan 1996:163–85).

From these and other studies the following conclusions may be drawn:

- In conventional training systems, the teaching cost is traditionally held to be a recurrent cost that is variable with the number of students in the system.
- In contrast, in distance training systems the cost of developing materials can be regarded as a fixed cost and can be written off over the life of the course. It follows that the more students using the materials, the lower the average cost per student, of the materials.
- At some point, and this depends on the costs of the choice of media, the distance system should become cheaper per unit of output than a traditional system.
- The use of face-to-face tuition tends to undermine the cost advantage of distance systems by reintroducing a cost element that is directly variable with student numbers.

- The number of dropouts in the system is crucial. Once the dropout level passes 50 per cent and moves towards 100 per cent, cost-effectiveness vanishes.
- If student support services are face-to-face and compulsory, the cost advantages of distance systems move back again towards those of conventional education. This has particular implications for group-based distance systems in the US and elsewhere.

In the 1970s it was shown that the average recurrent cost for a full-time undergraduate at the OUUK was less than one-third the cost at a campus university, and that the cost of a graduate was less than half. Nearly two decades later, Peters and Daniel (1994) showed that cost comparisons were still in favour of the OUUK.

Can the distance systems hold their market?

The fundamental principle in the research summarised in this chapter is that expenditure on technology by distance systems, whether on the web or not, must not be excessive. The choice of a high-cost medium, like television production, introduces permanent cost-inducing variables into the system.

The challenges facing designers of distance training in the years to come are:

- The initial investment in establishing distance systems, whether electronic or not, prior to the enrolment of any students is likely to be significant, and, on the whole, more costly than is the case with conventional systems.
- Distance systems, like industries, have high capital investment in the production of courses; conventional education is labour intensive.
- Distance systems can greatly increase student volumes without structural changes, and can do this with relative rapidity.
- If a number of cost-inducing variables are controlled, student numbers can be increased without proportionate increases in costs.

This chapter has provided a quantification of the public distance training market in a large part of one continent and indicators of its division among the four major stakeholders. It seems unlikely that all the stakeholders will maintain their share of the industry market indicated in this chapter. Factors which will impact on market share in the new century include the move to the web, the arrival of new players into the distance learning field, the role of group-based distance systems of the Electronics Revolution, and the march of communications and information technologies.

9 The coming of the Internet

A mature field

There is now little doubt that the World Wide Web is the most successful educational tool to have appeared in a long time. It combines and integrates text, audio and video with interaction among participants. It can be used on a global scale and is platform independent. While largely an asynchronous medium, it can also be used for synchronous events. It is not surprising, therefore, that trainers, lecturers, distance education providers and teaching institutions at all levels are increasingly using the World Wide Web as a medium for course provision (Mason 1998).

By 1998 the provision of education and training on the internet and on the World Wide Web was already a mature field of distance training provision. This was demonstrated by the European Commission project, *Courses on the Internet: Surveys, Analyses, Evaluation, Recommendations* (CISAER), published on the net at http://www.nki.no/~morten/cisaer.

In surveying and analysing training provision on the World Wide Web, this project carried out a series of 80 in-depth interviews in mid-1998, with world leaders in virtual education. These experts, from a wide range of countries, talked in long distance telephone interviews with confidence and expertise on issues of server provision, of kernel choice and of system design. They analysed changes in systems and systems design, when one moved from 200 students on the web, to 2,000 students on the web, to 20,000 students on the web.

There could be no doubt from these interviews and the surveys published on the CISAER website, that by 1998 training on the World Wide Web was a mature and professional field of provision, with its own rules, structures, achievements and literature.

This is surprising because Collis (1996) in her *Telelearning in a Digital World: The Future of Distance Learning* was able to identify the origins of this field of training provision, to the period from late 1994 to early 1995.

By 1997, Fritsch, in Germany, had started the analysis of a new training market. He identified students who:

- spent more than 20 hours a week working in front of a screen;
- had a company or university link to the internet;

- could write or edit a page in html;
- wanted to be trained in front of their screen.

It seems remarkable that, by 1997, there was a new market of people who spent most of their day in front of a computer screen and wanted to be trained in front of their screen, too.

Systematic evaluation began early too. Boshier, a professor of adult education at the University of British Columbia, tells how he led a team of researchers to comb the web between 15 February 1997 and 10 April 1997 for courses. His findings, already published in major articles in *Distance Education* in 1997 and 1998, under the jazzy titles 'Best and Worst Dressed Web Courses: Strutting into the Twenty-first Century in Comfort and Style' and 'World Wide America? Think Globally, Click Locally', state:

> Web courses are constructed as the answer to fiscal crises evoked by neo-liberal restructuring. They are also touted as an anarchist exemplar of 'de-schooling' as envisaged by Ivan Illich. The trouble is, some courses are vastly under-dressed and merely attempt to display a face-to-face course on-line. At the other extreme are those laced with links, animation and more than enough glitter and glam to make Liberace wince. In this study the authors employed a 43-item coding schedule to examine the accessibility, opportunities for interaction and attractiveness of 127 courses on the web. (1997:327)

and:

> The web assists the globalisation process but, as Canadians, we are apprehensive about US dominance. The problem will partly be overcome as more non-American sites are posted and search engines deployed. In the meantime, educators outside the US committed to building their own nation and preserving its culture and sense of itself, should think about how to develop local web resources so as to rely less on the US. (1998:121)

Course databases

By late 1999, a catalogue of on-line courses at TeleEducation, New Brunswick had reached 17,000 entries out of their global estimate of 30,000 courses available.

The 17,000 entries are listed on the web (see Figure 9.1, p. 92).

Each of the 17,000 courses in the catalogue was provided with a 54-category analysis at http://courses.telecampus.edu (see Figure 9.2, p. 92).

This listing of on-line courses is only one of the many available, which would include, Berlin Online Courses, Texas Global Learning, and Corrigan's *CASO's Internet University: Your Guide to Online College Courses* (1998) with 3,250 entries

TeleEducation, New Brunswick is hopeful that all on-line courses can eventually be catalogued in their database. This is because of the agreement between the

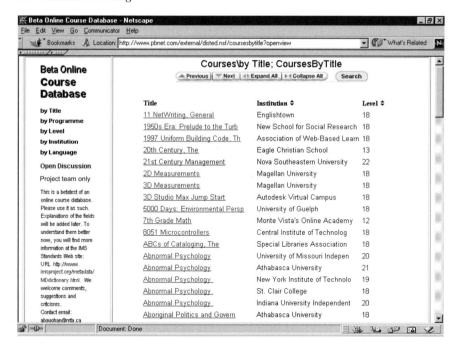

Figure 9.1 Listing of 17,000 on-line courses by TeleEducation, New Brunswick

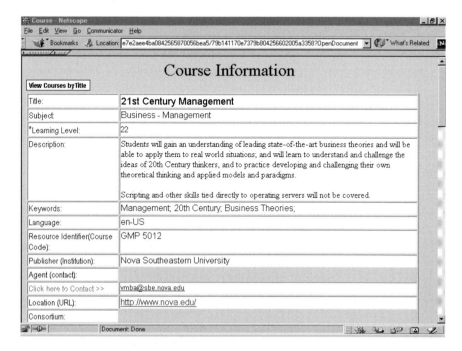

Figure 9.2 Start of a 54-category analysis in TeleEducation, New Brunswick database

Ariadne Agency of the European Commission and IMS in the US, to accept joint standards, so that in future the spiders of the database compilers can search for all courses on the web as it becomes in everyone's interest to follow the new agreed standards.

As the new millennium dawns, there is a rich array of virtual universities, virtual universities developed by conventional universities, virtual universities or training centres developed by international corporations, offering courses both in-house and courses for the public.

This constitutes an unprecedented development of a whole new area of distance training provision in the years 1995 to 1999.

Listservs

The theoretical analysis and academic foundations of the new field of web-based distance training were being analysed in a number of listservs. In the preparation for this book about 10,000 contributions to the Distance Education On-line Symposium (DEOS), a listserv hosted on a server at Pennsylvania State University in America, were studied.

This listserv received about 30 e-mails per day during the period mid-1998 to mid-1999. All of them were about distance education, and a considerable number of them were about web-based training. Most were well-informed. Most were American. Although they focused on the electronic developments of distance education, including education by satellite and education by videoconferencing, a considerable and growing volume was about education on the World Wide Web.

Contributors discussed, with technical and didactical competence, a range of issues which, in the period mentioned, contained these threads:

- What makes a web-based course successful?
- Copyright of electronic materials.
- Do virtual learners teach themselves?
- Distance education class sizes.
- The cost of teaching on the web.
- *Dreamweaver* versus *Front Page*.
- Certification of web-based courses.
- Cheating in web-based courses.
- What are the strengths of TopClass and how does it compare to WebCT™?

The theoretical underpinnings of training on the web are being developed on the net.

Seamless interfaces

Is the new area of web-based training to be regarded as a form of conventional education, or a form of distance education, or does it constitute a new sector of educational endeavour and a new field of educational research?

The position taken up here is that web-based education is best regarded as a subset of distance education and that the skills, literature, and practical management decisions that have been developed in the form of educational provision known as 'distance education', will be applicable *mutatis mutandis* to web-based education. It also follows that the literature on the field of educational research known as distance education, is of value for those embarking on training on the web.

Not all would agree.

In her *Telelearning in a Digital World: The Future of Distance Learning*, Collis sees the WWW as an innovation in education worldwide which will mean children in schools will be taught on the web, students who travel daily to universities will be taught on the web as well as, or instead of, the lecture theatre, students at work will be taught on the web, students at home will be taught on the web, and students globally will be taught on the web.

In spite of the position of Collis and others who share similar positions to hers, it is considered here that the legal distinctions outlined in this book should be decisive. A student contracts with a conventional school, college, or university to attend that institution, to join its community of students, and to receive its certificate or diploma or degree. Whether this student receives the qualification by attending classes or lectures, working in the library, or the laboratory, or at a computer screen, or on the WWW, depends on the legal requirements stipulated in the statutes of the institution.

Distance education is different. The student legally chooses not to attend the institution, or is unable to (for example, if in prison), or chooses not to (for example, if disabled), and requires the institution to award him or her its certificate or diploma or degree without joining its community of scholars. There need, in fact, be no physical institution for the student to attend in distance training, because the educational environment, in which the teaching–learning interaction takes place, is artificially created.

Whether this student receives the qualification by studying printed materials, or audio materials, or video materials, or computer materials, or on the WWW, and whether the student studies at an airport, or at home, or at work, and whether communication between students is compulsory or optional, face-to-face or electronic, depends on the didactic and administrative decisions made by the institution.

The structures presented in this study might be presented diagrammatically (see Figure 9.3).

In spite of the possibility of synchronous WWW didactic interaction, it is considered that web-based training is predominantly an individual-based form of educational provision. In spite of the possibility of full-time, on-campus students using the web for part of their degree, it is considered that web-based training can be accommodated within the existing structures of distance training, and there appears to be no necessity for the development of a new sector of educational endeavour or a new field of educational research.

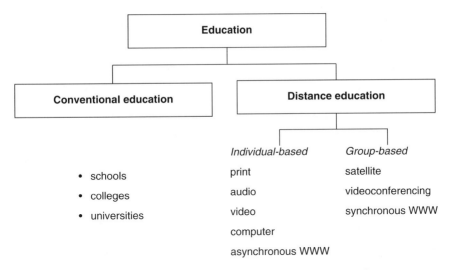

Figure 9.3 Relationship between web-based training and distance education

'Web-based training is better than traditional training'

In early 1998 newspapers worldwide carried an article claiming that 'web-based training is better than traditional training'.

Reuters had syndicated an article about the research of Professor Jerald G. Schutte of California State University on web-based training. Professor Schutte had proved, the press reported, that students on the web score 20 per cent better than students in traditional universities.

Professor Schutte reports his finding thus:

> Students in a Social Statistics course at California State University, Northridge, were randomly divided into two groups, one taught in a traditional classroom and the other taught virtually on the World Wide Web. Text, lectures and exams were standardised between the conditions. Contrary to the proposed hypotheses, quantitative results demonstrated the virtual class scored an average of 20 per cent higher than the traditional class on both examinations. (http://www.csun.edu/sociology/virexp.htm)

The syndicated report was widely used, and is often referred to, because of its striking claims.

Other claims abound:

> If the growing numbers of educators, book publishers and entrepreneurs are right, going to school will increasingly mean going online because training and education are already booming on the web.
>
> While entertainment-oriented web sites continue to wrestle with revenue models, educational sites are providing a familiar service, only improved by

the web's inherent advantages in terms of geography and time. Students can learn whenever they want, wherever they want, and only what they want. (http://www.webreview.com/97/01/31/feature/index.html)

These presentations carry forecasts and threats that either or both conventional education and distance education are about to be swamped by web-based education. Invariably these claims show little or no familiarity with the literature, little or no familiarity with educational success or failure at a distance in the past, and little or no research to justify the claims made: but they can be highly influential. Placing these claims in the context of the distance training literature allows us a framework for evaluation.

Programme taxonomy

Should internet courses be referred to as on-line courses or virtual courses or internet courses or web-based courses? These different terms suggest different approaches.

On-line course is a popular term except in those countries where on-line students must pay money to their telecom provider for every minute that they are on-line. The thought of mounting telephone bills, plus VAT, makes the idea of studying on-line unattractive.

A virtual training system, or virtual university, comprises an electronic classroom from which the class is taught, a network of electronic classrooms at which the students are present, and the satellite, microwave or cable linkages between them.

Courses on the net predated courses on the web. In their simplest form at the start of the 1990s they comprised printed materials posted to the students, plus an e-mail address for student to institution communication. Other possibilities (some of them not very feasible) which would be internet, but not WWW, courses include:

- e-mail-based courses
- a MOO (multi-user oriented object)
- a MUD (multi-user dungeon)
- audiographics courses
- courses using streaming non-WWW video, like CU-SeeMe, Microsoft NetMeeting, or some other internet conferencing software
- telnet-based communication
- a threaded conference using a non-WWW software.

Web-based courses would normally have at least one of these facilities:

- access to course resources
- student interaction with tutor or fellow students
- access to or submission of assignments
- activities/simulations/exercises.

Thus a web-based course can be defined as a course that uses the WWW of which the basic component is the web page. In a training course this could be either basic html, or forms using CGI (computer-generated images), or the possibility of links, or the possibility of plug-ins (Director, Acrobat, Powerpoint), or the possibility of other multimedia.

The course, therefore, is accessed through a WWW browser. This raises the question of how the course gets to the browser. It could be via the internet, or on a CD-Rom, or by an intranet, or data line.

McGreal's database

In the development of the TeleEducation, New Brunswick database of on-line courses, McGreal (1999) performed a useful function by publishing on the web his categories for inclusion and exclusion. He analyses 17 types of on-line course.

His database is built from courses that can be followed completely on-line. Excluded from McGreal's database are courses that have no on-line component or courses which require residency or attendance.

This does not mean that all course materials need to be on-line. Like any distance training course, books, CD-Roms, video and/or audio and laboratory materials can be shipped out to students and examinations taken at local institutions or testing centres.

Within this context McGreal presents his list of categories of courses and programmes on the internet as a continuum.

Courses with no, or limited, availability for distance training:

1 Classroom-based courses with no on-line features (advertised on-line).
2 Classroom-based courses with some materials available on-line.
3 Classroom-based courses that integrate on-line materials.
4 On-campus courses that are on-line but are not available to distance students.
5 On-campus courses that offer limited access to students at a distance (often limited to one region).
6 Teleconferencing courses where students must participate from specified learning centres.

The first six groupings represent the majority of courses at present advertised as available for study on the internet. They do not qualify for inclusion in McGreal's database. All require residency, either on a university campus or at a learning centre.

The virtual university in Barcelona, the Universitat Oberta de Catalunya, is excluded because of its compulsory attendance stipulations (see Chapter 6). Many universities in Finland, Sweden and Denmark claim that their WWW courses are under-represented in this database, but this is due to what promoters of the web call the old, elitist requirements of European universities to require compulsory attendance (see Chapter 12).

Correspondence courses (print, audio and video tapes, software):

7 Print-based correspondence courses using the postal system with minimal student support.

8   Print-based correspondence courses with continuing access to a tutor by telephone.

These would not be included in the TeleEducation database either, as they are not available on-line. Thus most open university courses and most proprietary distance training courses do not figure because, strangely, they do not allow, or do not as yet allow, e-mail assignment submission and/or interaction.

McGreal's database is therefore built up of his categories 9 to 17:

On-line distance training courses:

9   Print-based correspondence courses also using e-mail for tutor access.
10   Correspondence courses with course content available on-line in electronic format.
11   CBT-based self-study courses with access on-line to an instructor.
12   CBT-based self-study courses with no instructor.

Computer-mediated conferencing (CMC)

These courses often include texts and sometimes include audio/video tapes, and computer software possibly including computer-based training courseware. Students may need to download and install client-side software to participate. Here, asynchronous communication is available with discussion packages, listservs or bulletin boards.

13   Courses that use e-mail for submission of assignments and private tutoring and e-mail lists or listservs for discussions and tutoring.
14   Courses that use CMC software for discussions as well as e-mail for submission of assignments and private tutoring.
15   CMC courses with all content, audio/video, and software available on-line; students can download and print out content or read it on-line.

Hypermedia on the World Wide Web

These courses can be followed on-line on the World Wide Web. They take advantage of the links to other relevant sites using subject trails and other techniques. These courses can be either text-based, and so available to students with low bandwidth connections, or they can include graphics and animations, that require a more powerful computer and higher bandwidth. This grouping includes synchronous communication.

16   Courses that use hypertext links and have all necessary course materials on-line.
17   Courses with hypermedia links with multimedia using Shockwave, Quicktime, or other applications.

Analysis

It is important to realise that McGreal's categories, like the rest of the analyses in this book, are non-judgemental. Analysis of provision is presented. There is no value judgement that one category is superior to another.

Various permutations of the taxonomy described are possible. For example any multimedia web course might also have a text component. A CMC (computer mediated communication) course could have some hypermedia links and a workbook. A print-based course could incorporate some multimedia courseware on a CD-Rom with hyperlinks to the World Wide Web.

Classification for this study

It is felt that McGreal's 17 levels of training on-line form an excellent tool, but are too complex for practical web-based training management. For readers who are new to the field, or for distance training institutions thinking of putting their courses on the web, a simpler classification is needed.

In what follows, five categories of web-based training are proposed.

Classification 1   Courses on the internet

Technical provision

Only publicity or information is on the WWW. No didactic use of http/html pages. E-mail provision. Student has no ISP link.

Didactic provision

Courses are developed and sent to the student on paper, or by CD-Rom, or by modem. E-mail contacts provided. Many US virtual universities and on-line corporate universities use systems similar to this.

Cost implications

The costs incurred include those for course development and for distributing the learning materials to students, and for student support services, including e-mail.

Classification 2   WWW on students' PCs

Technical provision

The system provides files or documents that students can download to their own PCs. Also e-mail contact address for technical support on downloading.

Didactic provision

This classification makes didactic use of the WWW. Learning materials are on the WWW and are downloadable. It is a form of electronic textbook.

Cost implications

There are server costs and some technical support costs, and some costs for provision of e-mail addresses. There are costs for distribution of learning materials to students and for student support services, including e-mail.

Classification 3 WWW courses on-line

Technical provision

Html material on-line. Materials structured to provide next/back and links to other materials. Graphics, questions and answers, assignment correction provided on-line.

Didactic provision

Materials are didactically structured and easy to follow. There is more structure for student progression, self-assessment and student interaction.

Cost implications

There are costs for a webmaster, staff or a consultant who can write html, PERL, and other scripts for passwords and for student interaction, graphics, and web design. Additional server space required and password controls.

Classification 4 WWW multimedia courses

Technical provision

A proprietary database management system, like WebCT™, is purchased, or the system designs one. Audio clips, video clips, simulations and full interactivity are provided. The system has conferencing structures for student interaction. May support videoconferencing with whiteboard facility.

Didactic provision

The system provides didactic interactivity. There is an increased range of student content, images and course type. Increased provision of student results, testing, tutoring and counselling.

Cost implications

Larger server costs for a server system of at least three servers. Automatic maintenance costs. Further costs for e-mail, tutoring and student correspondence as in any distance training course. Development costs for course material.

Classification 5   WWW dynamic multimedia courses

Technical provision

Dynamic course content; Java; advanced simulations; large database construction; extension of database management system to allow it to integrate fully with a dedicated web server; personalisation of courses.

Didactic provision

Creation of an on-line community. Possible to address individual preferences and needs. Sophisticated course content and presentation.

Cost implications

High-end server for database. Java specialist needed and full-time maintenance staff. System is in charge of its own server. Regular upgrades of database software to ensure speed and stability. There are the usual costs for distributing the learning materials to students, and for student support services, including e-mail.

Analysis of server provision

Training on the web provides new challenges to training providers, whether they train face-to-face in training centres or colleges, or whether they teach at a distance.

They are faced with a range of technical issues and computing strategies with which training institutions may not be familiar, and for which the qualifications of staff and management may not be sufficient. They are faced with a shift from didactic to technical emphasis for which they may be unprepared. To have a training system, with student interaction and recording of student data, on the web, institutions are faced with three areas of decision making:

- analysis of server provision
- analysis of kernel provision
- analysis of kernel providers.

The answers will vary for systems with:

- 200 students on the web
- 2,000 students on the web
- 20,000 students on the web.

The issues on server provision mean a choice of:

- renting space on a server
- leasing a server
- purchasing a server or set of servers.

Renting space on a server

At the time of writing, and from certain suppliers, 100 mb (megabyte) can be bought for €/$100, plus a monthly rental fee of €/$25. For a larger system 1 gb (gigabyte) can be purchased for an initial €/$500, plus the monthly fee.

The advantages are that one has a system for little outlay, and limited backup responsibility for the institution.

The disadvantages are that it would not be fast and that, although the institution has an account on a box, so do, perhaps, 1,000 others. The needs of the others might get priority from the server owner and if the other renters should log on at the same time, the system will be too slow for its students. If the server crashes one might get it back up within two to three days. There is not enough power or complexity for the students, and this solution should not be considered for 2,000 or 20,000 students.

Leasing a server

One can lease a server from a provider like Digiweb. At the time of writing, and from certain providers, €/$500 is the cost of the domain name, and €/$250 per month leasing fee, with adequate technical support from the server provider plus additional technical support from one's own system. This would be suitable for 200 or 2,000 students.

Buying a server or a set of servers

At the time of writing, and from certain vendors, the server hardware could cost from €/$2,000 to €/$15,000, plus the €/$500 subscription for the domain name, plus a budget of €/$15,000 per year for maintenance with a dedicated staff member, or members, providing continuous technical support.

This solution is suitable for 200 to 20,000 students. Renting space on a server cannot reasonably handle 20,000 students. 20,000 students on a leased server(s) could be done, but costs can get very high.

For 20,000 students, a training system cannot afford to rely on a provider, however competent. There would, in any case, probably be problems with the leasing company who might want to know why there was so much traffic on their server. As most companies that lease servers are American, and it is difficult to contact them before 08.00 their time, the leasing option can be problematical for non-American systems.

Analysis of kernel provision

Institutions faced with the decision to transfer some or all of their face-to-face and/or distance training provision to the web, face further choices on the shell or kernel to run their web-based training system. These decisions have far-reaching implications for the didactic strategies of the institution, and for the continuing costs of the training system.

There are three options:

- rent a kernel from one of the leading providers
- adapt an existing kernel for use in one's own system
- develop one's own system.

Renting a kernel

This is the popular solution, with most major providers listing on their web site the universities and training institutions who have installed their system. Most systems, at the time of writing, are costed on a per student licence up to a certain total, after which an unlimited licence is bought.

The advantages are that an institution gets a full training system with extensive functionality both for course development and student support services, plus a database for student records and interactivity. The costs and competencies for writing and maintaining the code for a complete system, and then continually developing it to meet developments in the market, will be beyond most institutions.

Adapting an existing kernel

Some commercial kernels can be customised and adapted to meet an institution's requirements. At the time of writing, some existing systems are claimed to be weak on audio, or video, or didactic quality. The advertised 'we will install your virtual university for you and have it up and running within 24 hours' may not suit all institutions.

Despite the fact that two of the current leading kernels are Canadian and Irish, much of the didactic structure is highly Americanised. Quizzes and chats are not everyone's concepts of a university degree. Excellent software is increasingly available, but may not be included in the kernel purchased.

Developing one's own system

A number of issues might suggest a university or training institution would write, develop and maintain its own system.

A university may claim it was already teaching on the net before the major proprietary systems became available, or its senate may claim that the university's charter did not envisage using some other university's system to teach. The functionality of proprietary kernels may not be adequate for local needs.

Systems that have the potential to move beyond 10,000 students will consider developing their own kernel. Major universities already have a look and feel to their web presence, and may insist that their courses on the web follow this design. Some proprietary kernels are not easily customised.

Analysis of kernel providers

When the choice is made to purchase a proprietary system, the institution needs to evaluate the range available. In-depth and balanced evaluations can be found on the web, but the range of criteria chosen in the reports may not be identical to the institution's needs. For instance in 1999 at http://www.umn.edn/, the University of Minnesota provided an evaluation of the Academos, ClassWeb, TopClass, WebCT™ systems, against these criteria:

- publication of information
- tools for interaction
- tools for assessment
- access to centralised resources
- ease of use
- technical features.

A major additional factor is cost. Some months later the market leaders appeared to have changed, with Lotus Notes joining TopClass and WebCT™ in a leading group for some evaluators.

Summary

The Norwegian scholar, Paulsen, sums up the discussion on the identity of courses on the web at http://www.nettskolen.com/kurs/0000-spice.homeside.html:

> There are many terms for online education. Some of them are: virtual education, Internet-based education, web-based education and education via computer-mediated communication. This programme uses a definition of on-line education, which is based on a well-known definition of distance education. Hence, online education is characterised by:
>
> - the separation of teachers and learners which distinguishes it from face-to-face education
> - the influence of an educational organisation which distinguishes it from self-study and private tutoring
> - the use of a computer network to present or distribute some educational content
> - the provision of two-way communication via a computer network so that students may benefit from communication with each other, teachers, and staff.

He adds his views of what web-based courses should strive to achieve:

> The program offers online education via the internet. It emphasises independence of time, space, and pace; features that are among the most cherished in online education. Hence, the program accepts continuous enrolment,

individual progression, and single course enrolment. This means that students can enrol whenever they want, they can decide their own progression schedule, and they do not need to enrol for more than one course.

Paulsen indicates student access advantages thus:

> All courses are offered online. This means that there is no need for students to travel or take part in any face-to-face sessions as long as they have access to the internet. All course communication could be conducted online via email and discussion forums. Further, the program emphasises asynchronous communication. Hence, there is no need to attend classes scheduled for certain days or specific hours. Further, the study guides are developed as web pages, which include course material, assignments, and links to international resources.

Conclusion

The role of web-based training as part of distance training at the start of the new millennium is already impressive. It is as well, however, to have a clear concept of what is being discussed when one talks of 'training on the web', as McGreal's 17 categories show. The position taken here is similar to McGreal's:

1 Courses on the web which fall within the definition of distance training developed in Chapter 4 of this book, are included within the concept of education learning in this book, but do-it-yourself packages, self-instruction courses, electronic teach-yourself-books on the net or web are not.
2 Secondly, the courses must be available to the public – thus private training, in-house company training on the net or web, or courses on an intranet, or courses in which the public cannot enrol are not included.
3 Presence on the web is insufficient for inclusion – there must be some didactic use of the web. At least one of the following, (i) student interaction with the institution or other students (ii) access to or submission of assignments (iii) access to course resources (iv) activities, simulations or exercises, should be web-based.
4 The focus of this book is not the study of students on-campus. Web or net courses offered to full-time, campus-based students are not included in the study.

The offering of courses for degree credit on the World Wide Web is a major development and the issue of its legitimacy justifies precise analysis.

10 Distance training on the World Wide Web

Design of a kernel

The first stage for a distance training system which wishes to teach on the WWW is to acquire a kernel, that is a system for developing WWW courses, offering them to students on the WWW, and teaching the WWW students, ideally, with a database for student records and results.

To be effective as a successful internet application for a distance course delivery system, the kernel should have a range of features: these will mirror the course development subsystem, the student support subsystem, and the student administration subsystem of a typical distance training institution.

Kernels can either be purchased, leased or developed by the distance training institution itself.

Among the range of features the kernel system should have are:

- Text – as most students learn by reading there is a requirement for the quality provision of text.
- Voice – some aspects of course material are best explained verbally, so the product will include an audio component.
- Moving image – some content, like the teaching of how diesel engines work, requires moving images, so there will be a moving image subsystem.
- Video – a video subsystem can be of value both for course development and for student services, so a kernel facility for video streaming over the Internet should be available.
- Internet telephone – the provision of student support using internet telephony needs to be investigated.
- Graphics – some content like the history of the world in the 1920s requires graphic presentation, and a comprehensive graphics package will be a feature of the system.
- Simulations – many exercises or Self-Assessment Questions would be simulations.
- Assignment submission – a structure for the submission of assignments to the system's computer any time of day or night.
- Assignment correction – instantly by the system's computer any time of day or night, any day of the year.

- Assignment feedback – instantly at any time of day or night by a personalised and customised letter from the system to the individual student.
- Student records – facility for cumulative records for certification and counselling.
- E-mail – a facility for student-to-institution interaction.
- Conference – a facility for student-to-student interaction which will remove the loneliness of studying at a distance.
- Bulletin board – a facility for institution-to-student(s) communication.

Thus a kernel comprises a range of didactic and technical services needed for a web-based training system. The services provided by the kernel are taken into the kernel domain of the institution. Then the kernel implementations are used to develop the courses and the courses are taught to students. This might be represented diagrammatically thus:

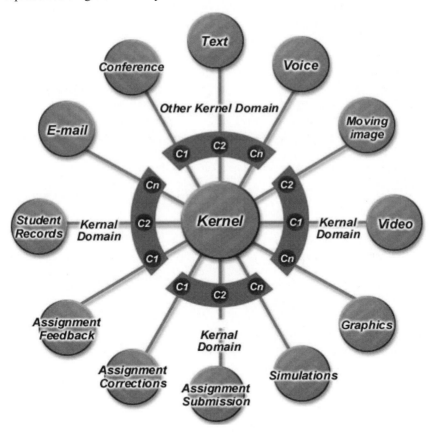

Figure 10.1 Design of a kernel for a web-based training system

This model of a completed kernel can now be compared with other kernel solutions.

WebCT™

There are a range of commercial kernels on the market including First Class, WebCT™, TopClass and others. At the time of writing, the WebCT™ kernel, developed by Goldberg at the University of British Columbia in Vancouver, is popular with distance training systems. It is appropriate, therefore, to analyse the WebCT™ kernel and contrast it with the kernel outline provided here. A screenshot of the WebCT™ kernel is provided by Goldberg at http://www.webct.com/webct/map/imagemap. html:

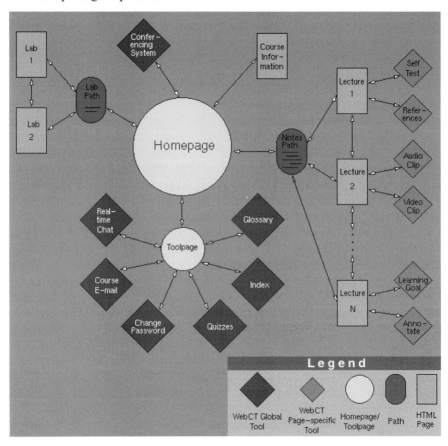

Figure 10.2 Design of a kernel for a web-based training system: WebCT™ solution. (Reproduced by permission of WebCT™.)

It can be seen that at the heart of the WebCT™ kernel is the homepage from which a close link is established to the toolpage. Briefly, the homepage deals with the content of the course and the toolpage deals with the administration of the courses.

The homepage is developed by a series of:

- paths
- html pages
- page-specific tools.

In distance education terms, these provide the course development part of the distance education didactic process. The paths lead from the homepage to the content of the course and to practical or laboratory sessions. The html pages provide the content of the course (lectures) and the content of the practical sessions (laboratories). The page-specific tools provide the functionality for the html pages of the lectures:

- self-testing (SAQs)
- reference (a list of sources of readings)
- audio clip (audio recordings)
- video clip (video recordings)
- learning goal (objectives)
- annotate (personal work area).

The homepage leads directly to a further range of functionality:

- course notes
- assignments
- course information
- using WebCT™
- bulletin board
- quizzes on-line
- student functions
- e-mail within course
- counter.

The toolpage leads to a range of global tools:

- real-time chat
- course e-mail
- change password
- quizzes
- index
- glossary
- conferencing system.

In distance education terms the toolpage could be considered to represent the student support services.

Using a system like WebCT™

If you go to a WebCT™ shop you will find several different UNIX versions and an NT version. You download a single compressed file to suit your system. WebCT™ is not available on CD-Rom as it is a web product and is not designed for CD usage. You download it, then you decompress it, then you install it with its own install programme, and then off you go. Typically it is a compressed file of 12 mb and can take about two hours to download. Decompressed it might be between 20 and 30 mb. When you have used it to develop your course and you try to use your course or to enrol students, a warning says that it 'is a non-licensed version'. You then buy a licence.

Evaluation

The major technical problem of a web-based training system, apart from bandwidth, is the design, structure and security of the management system. For any large number of students the database is crucial.

The central system problem is storing data and getting it back. This means adding students, deleting students, assigning different functionality to different students.

Thus the kernel is a database system and a management system with the system design: the setting up of the files, directories and structures together with the records that are kept.

System management

A successful kernel for web-based training will provide the two characteristic subsystems: course development and student support services, with the course development process usually being completed before the course is studied by students. The student support services half of the distance training process is the structures that the institution puts in place to support the student from enrolment to examination. It also contributes to the avoidance of avoidable drop-out.

It is claimed that it is the provision of both subsystems, the course development subsystem and the student support subsystem, that distinguishes distance education from self-study, or study from CD-Roms, and which justifies the awarding of university degrees and nationally-recognised training diplomas and certificates by distance education institutions.

Goldberg's WebCT™ design corresponds precisely to these concerns. The homepage with its Notes path and Lab path is analogous to the course development subsystem of a distance training design. It has rich functionality and provides, not only Lecture 1, Lecture 2, Lecture n, for the content of the course, but also Lab 1, Lab 2, Lab n, for practical applications and exercises on the content.

The toolpage, on the other hand, is an implementation of the student support services of a distance system and provides support during the period of study. In spite of the use of terminology like 'chat' and 'quizzes', it provides the required creation of the educational milieu in which the teaching/learning process takes place, and justifies the award of degrees, diplomas and certificates for successful study on the web.

Thus a kernel for distance training is a set of servers which provide the various services required by the different kernel applications by using open source or purchased or home-developed scripts and software.

The WWW in practice

Institutions who wish to change their training from either face-to-face training in training centres or colleges, or from non-electronic distance training, will need to address a range of new didactic and technical issues, a selection of which are presented here.

Learning and design theory

The adaptation of learning theory to the student seated in front of his or her screen for the length of the training programme is a major concern. The presentation of the course content on the computer screen, and the application to training on the WWW of the findings of Schneiderman (1992) and others, on designing the user interface and strategies for effective human–computer interaction, raise important issues.

These include:

- rules of dialogue design
- guidelines for data display
- guidelines for data entry
- menu selection and form-filling
- interaction devices
- response time and display rate
- screen design and colour
- multiple window strategies
- synchronous and asynchronous interactions
- on-line help.

Schneiderman (1992:72) gives his eight golden rules for interface design as: strive for consistency; enable frequent users to use shortcuts; offer informative feedback; design dialogues to yield closure; offer single error handling; permit easy reversal of actions; support internal locus of control; reduce short-term memory load.

Hardware and software purchase

Distance training systems changing to the WWW need to make decisions on the purchase or renting of servers; the purchase or design of kernels; staffing for system and/or server maintenance and for code writing or adaptation; choice of browser, e-mail systems, bulletin boards, conference packages, multimedia on the web, streaming audio and/or video, database interfaces.

Student support services

Decisions need to be made, and systems established, for on-line or off-line course advertising, student application, student enrolment, payment of fees, student counselling, student tutoring, resource facilities, library facilities.

Systems need to be designed for on-line or off-line student interaction and for synchronous or asynchronous student events. Paulsen (1999) provides a useful summary, shown in Figure 10.3.

Student assessment

The goal here will be to provide assignment submission to the institution's server any time of day or night, any day of the year, even public holidays. Assignment correction will be immediately done by the institution's computer systems.

The design of questions for web-based assessment is a specialised skill. One of the normal structures for assignments, that of ticking one of four boxes, needs scientific assignment design to achieve academic credibility. The best designs will set the students reflecting for 20 minutes or more, send them back to the course content, or to additional textbooks, before the decision on which box to tick can be made.

Assignment feedback will be in the form of a personalised, customised letter to the student, praising his or her success, pointing out the reasons for error, and suggesting paths for further improvement. This feedback will be generated from data banks assiduously prepared and triggered by the varying results received from the student. Government privacy legislation may block some of these procedures in certain countries.

Student interaction

Student interaction will be provided by e-mail, bulletin boards, conference packages and threaded discussions. Shared computer applications, audioconferencing and videoconferencing are also possible.

The American use of the term 'chatting' for student-to-student interaction on the web seems unfortunate, as school students are normally punished for chatting. The emphasis on interactivity and alternative hyperlinked paths through courses and their justification from the viewpoint of cognitivist psychology may also be misplaced. The main market for web-based training for adults off-campus will probably differ little from distance training: taxpayers who are fully-employed and require the shortest path from enrolment to examination and have little interest in chatting.

Instructional strategies

The progression from face-to-face training, to distance training, to training on the web sees a focus on graphics, animation, audio and video, simulations, virtual worlds on the web, linked to non-web materials like textbooks, CDs, floppy disks and printed notes.

Methods:	One-to-web	One-to-one	One-to-many	Many-to-many
Techniques:	• On-line databases • On-line journals • On-line applications • Software libraries • On-line interest groups • Interviews	• Learning contract • Apprenticeships • Internships • Correspondence studies	• Lectures • Symposiums • Skits	• Debates • Simulations or games • Role plays • Case studies • Discussion groups • Transcript-based assignments • Brainstorming • Delphi techniques • Nominal group techniques • Forums • Project groups
Devices:	On-line resources	E-mail	Bulletin board	Computer conferencing

Figure 10.3 Dimensions of student interaction in web courseware (Paulsen 1999)

The use of (and purchase by the web-based training institution of the rights to) reference articles on the internet is a vital new institutional strategy for the web. Articles that, even five years ago, were essential course reading but only to be found by the inter-library loan of obscure journals, can now be made available on-line to enrolled students and read on screen or printed out.

Security and firewalls

Institutions initiating courses on the web will need to pay close attention to security. Although it is true that some institutions, like the International Management College (IMC) of Buckingham, England, put their courses on the net for all to see and study, most institutions password their courses and only issue passwords to students on the payment of course fees.

Security systems need to cover not only access to courses but also access to student records, results and interaction. Experience shows that students forget their passwords and multiple passwords for multiple enrolments in courses in differing areas cause logistical difficulties.

International corporations with heavily firewalled intranets and strict policies about the possibility of punching holes through their firewall to the internet, face further problems. Security provision for staff members from around the world to study on the web, must not lead the web-based students to sensitive data to which they would not otherwise have authorisation. If these corporations wish to sell their web-based courses to the general public, the firewalling problems become more acute.

Staffing

The distance training institutions moving to the web will need to hire or contract staff with new skills. Experience of html, PERL, CGI scripts, Java and Javascript may be needed. Although small systems may run by renting a spot on a server from a server provider, and eventually a whole server, once the enrolment on the web goes beyond 10,000 the institution will need qualified technicians to purchase, configure and maintain their own servers.

Similarly a small system may run on a kernel like WebCT™ or TopClass or the range of other proprietary kernels available, but systems with 10,000 students on the web will probably want to design, trial, and maintain their own system with their own staff.

Remuneration of staff in web-based systems has been a frequent thread on listserv discussions. The recurring distance training problem of who decides the final format of the course, the academic or the television producer (where the academic is not the producer) can rear its head again; as can the problem of whether they both get paid the same. Copyright and intellectual property ownership rights may be even more important than in distance training.

Solutions

Distance training institutions will find a rich variety of virtual training and virtual university courses on the web, which address the concerns listed above and provide models for analysis.

A screenshot of a recent course on information and communication technologies for SMEs (small and medium-sized enterprises) called 'Communication for the New Millennium' is given as an example:

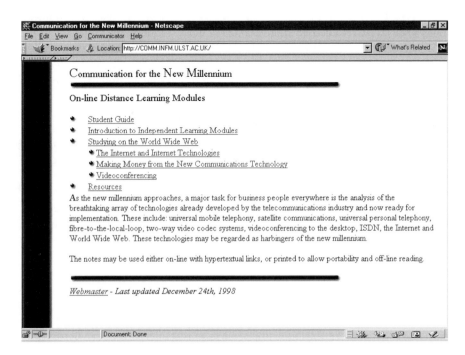

Figure 10.4 Example of a web-based training course

A recent analysis by Collis and Peters (1999) sees asynchronous video on the WWW as a solution:

> From the perspectives of efficiency and flexibility, the capability now becoming increasingly available for compressing and streaming video and making the video available via an ordinary WWW browser (with appropriate viewers) is a major step forward in overcoming usage problems. Assuming the video segments are available, and copyright issues are appropriately handled (the same problems that confront video use in videotape or CD-Rom form), the segments can be accessed via a WWW browser using streaming technology from wherever the user has adequate network access, and whenever the user wishes.

In training on the WWW, the solutions for young students with access to high technology, enrolled on-campus, may differ from those of the busy adult at home or the manager studying in her office.

Individualisation

Some scholars see in distance training on the WWW a possible solution to the age-old problem of streaming: teaching students of differing abilities in the same group which sometimes means that weak students learn less than they should. They want the course to be individualised at the student's browser, so that each student downloads a different course attuned to his or her individual needs.

When distance education systems are linked to advanced level computer facilities, the individualisation of student learning can finally be addressed. Institutions can build a picture of the characteristics of the student from the enrolment forms, from interviews, from communications, from tests taken, until it has a comprehensive analysis of the individual capabilities of the students.

The institution then can write each paragraph or section of the next course at three or more different levels. When the different versions of the course are fed into the computer, it is possible to punch out multiple versions of the same course for the same award, adapted to the needs of the individual student.

Language learning skills impact greatly on the ability of students to learn. In on-line distance training, however, it is possible to take a 100-word sample of a student's linguistic ability and sample it against the lexical coefficients of the national language thesaurus to punch out courses which eliminate vocabulary that is not within the student's range.

Evaluation

In 1976 Hawkridge published an article on the evolution of the replacement of the teacher by the teaching machine, under the dramatic title 'Next Year, Jerusalem! The Rise of Educational Technology'. The author traced this development from programmed learning machines, to the systems approach to learning, to audiovisual aids, to multimedia systems design. Will the web provide the ultimate teaching machine? Do virtual students teach themselves? Is the WWW a final solution? These are the questions that distance educators need to address at the turn of the millennium.

Any evaluation will have as its background the failure of many of the technologies proposed for distance training in the past, to deliver cost-effective course enrolments for distance systems which make money. The impact of the new mobile telephone and computer structures on the net and the web will be crucial in the early years of the new century. The swing towards group-based solutions with the electronics technologies of the 1980s may swing back towards the student as an individual studying alone on the World Wide Web.

A paradigm shift?

One hesitates to use the term 'a paradigm shift' of the arrival of yet another new technology in a field where it has been frequently used of false dawns and Jerusalems still to come.

For distance training institutions and their staff, nonetheless, there are serious challenges in the developments of training on the web. For the first time in the history of distance training, staff will be confronted with training provision for which a recent BSc in computing is more valuable than a degree or diploma in education and training. *This* is a paradigm shift.

11 Methodology

Global synthesis

An invitation to present a keynote address on a global overview of distance systems at the end of the second millennium, to the International Distance Education Conference in Shanghai at Easter 1998, created the need for a methodology that would enable all instances of a whole sector of education and training provision to be analysed.

Research and publication over a 20-year period had led to the collection of a great deal of data on distance systems worldwide at all levels:

- children's distance education
- distance training for vocational and professional qualifications
- corporate distance training
- university-level distance education systems
- systems on the net and the web.

Periods of work in distance systems at various levels in systems in the US, French-speaking Canada, English-speaking Canada, France, China, Italy, Germany, Ireland and England had resulted in the accumulation of a great amount of experiential data about the day-to-day running of these systems.

Contracts for the development of postgraduate degrees in distance education, or contributions to the development of postgraduate courses in distance education, at the University of South Australia, the University of Cosenza, the University of New England at Northern Rivers, the Télé-Université in Quebec, and the University of Surrey, necessitated analysis of the theory and practice of distance systems worldwide.

The issues

Various issues needed to be addressed. The two modes of distance education – group-based systems and individual-based systems – had not been identified; the richness of the field was little understood; few scholars had compared adequate data from China, from the US, from Europe and from the rest of the world.

The interfaces between teaching at a distance and teaching face-to-face at a distance had not really been addressed. The interfaces between the technologies of the Industrial Revolution and the Electronics Revolution needed further analysis. Above all, the failure of scholars and administrators, outside the US, to understand what the term *distance learning* meant there and on the web, really needed to be addressed. In like manner the failure of American scholars to realise that what they meant by *distance learning* had similarities with systems in China, but very little with European and English-speaking systems worldwide, was surprising.

The solution was to present the sector in its global context, as in Chapter 1 of this book, with a major division being made between group-based systems and individual-based systems. Within the group-based systems, it was decided that the full-time provision by the *Dianda* system in China warranted a category to itself, even though some scholars have queried the validity of dividing systems between full-time students and part-time students.

Systems aimed at individuals were also divided into two categories: those which prepared learning materials for the distance students and those systems which chose not to prepare learning materials but just handed out a curriculum guide, reading lists, and previous examination papers.

There are some scholars who would eliminate the Chinese examination system, the University of South Africa (UNISA) in the first half of the twentieth century, and the University of London external degree from their definition of distance education and training. It seemed inappropriate to eliminate these major systems, especially as the University of London external degree has been providing qualifications at a distance, globally, since the 1840s.

The placing of courses on the World Wide Web, within the synthesis, clearly posed problems. WWW courses were regarded as an electronic form of distance training, which was individualised, isolating the student in front of his or her screen, with the possibility that synchronous events could take place. It was decided, therefore, to consider web-based systems among the individual-based distance training systems with pre-prepared materials.

Census studies

The global synthesis provided in Chapter 1 gives a reader an overall view of a sector of training provision. This, however, was inadequate for the purposes of this book, which wished to present this whole field of educational endeavour as a harbinger of the new millennium and as a basis for taking stock of provision for the twenty-first century. For this purpose a census was needed, as statistical projections, or analyses of samples, were considered inadequate for the purpose of stocktaking.

It is often said that it is difficult to get statistical data on conventional face-to-face training in colleges and training centres, because not all governments collect and publish data in the same form on the complex world of vocational and technical and professional training systems. Statistics on university education are generally considered to be more precise.

It has also been said that collecting and analysing data on *distance* vocational, technical and professional training systems would be even more difficult than collecting data on *conventional*, face-to-face, instructor-led systems. On the whole, this is true, because distance students, in the main, study in the anonymity of their own houses, and do not attend the training centres that conventional training students do.

A methodology was required that would accurately analyse and quantify a complex field spread over the whole world. At once, a decision was made to limit the census to the countries of the EU, thus constructing a database for nearly the whole of a continent as an accurate presentation of the sector. If the methodology chosen proved successful, then other scholars might repeat the study for other continents.

The Delphi methodology

Fortunately, such a methodology is available. The Delphi method developed by Professor Norman C. Dalkey and his associates, at the University of Southern California, at Los Angeles, in the mid- to late 1960s, and then justified in empirical studies in the 1970s and later, is designed for: the solution of complex problems, in which no researcher or research institute has the data required, and in which a range of persons has a part of the data required.

Dalkey, in 1969, presented his methodology thus:

> The Delphi method is a set of procedures for formulating a group judgement for subject matter where precise information is lacking. In general, the procedure consists of obtaining individual answers to pre-formulated questions either by questionnaire or by some other formal communication technique; iterating the questionnaire one or more times where the information feedback between rounds is carefully controlled by the exercise manager; taking as the group response a statistical aggregate of the final answers.
>
> In previous studies it has been shown that the Delphi procedures led to increased accuracy of group responses more often than not, and that both the spread of answers (standard deviation of responses on a given question) and a self-rating index (average of individual self-ratings on a given question) are valid indicators of the mean accuracy of group responses.
>
> *Anonymous response*
> Opinions of members of the group are obtained by formal questionnaire.
>
> *Iteration and controlled feedback*
> Interaction is effected by a systematic exercise conducted in several iterations with carefully controlled feedback between rounds.
>
> *Statistical group response*
> The group opinion is defined as an appropriate aggregate of individual opinions on the final round.

These features are designed to minimise the biasing effects of dominant individuals or irrelevant communications and of group pressure towards conformity (Dalkey 1969).

Much of the early evaluation of the Delphi methodology was conducted by Dalkey and his associates, at the RAND Corporation in California, in the spring of 1968 and the main results were communicated in his publications.

Application

In practice, this study used the Delphi methodology by dividing the statistics to be established into 64 cells. Statistics are first divided into 16 national groupings, with two groupings for Belgium, and each national group is divided into the four sectors which research in this field, prior to the study, had shown were characteristic of national distance education systems:

- the distance teaching university
- distance education courses from conventional universities
- government provision at further education level
- proprietary provision at further education level.

It is accepted that the categories are not totally exclusive and that, in theory, it is possible to include a structure that might be outside the four structures chosen. In practice, however, it was felt that each citizen enrolled in a distance-training course could, in fact, be allocated to one of the four categories.

The goal was, therefore, to find four experts in each of the 16 national systems. It was felt that a grouping of four experts, each of whom was an expert in his or her own section, and all of whom were experts on the national scene, was the ideal for establishing accurate statistical and financial data, if such experts could be identified and if they agreed to participate.

Procedure

This is a census study and a market observatory of a field of educational endeavour. The central requirement of a study of this nature is that the phenomenon be measurable. It is considered that the category, 'students studying at a distance' is capable of measurement, though there are real difficulties of interpretation and practice in the UK and, to a lesser extent, the Scandinavian countries.

It was felt that by using a scientific definition instrument, students who choose not to, or are not able to, attend the training centres, the schools, the colleges, the universities of the EU, can be identified and counted and that this is a socio-economic phenomenon of such importance that the effort required to quantify it is valid.

The definition instrument used in this study is that reproduced in the third edition of *Foundations of Distance Education*. It is considered a definition instrument of sufficient precision, so that students who study in a distance training system can be identified from those who study in some other form of training provision.

Using this instrument, experts were allocated to the 64 cells into which the EU was divided for the purposes of this study. The experts were asked to identify for their cells the number of educational institutions which provided distance training, and this data was put through three iterations.

The next stage was to identify the number of enrolments in each institution in each cell, for a one-year period, counting only those students who enrolled for the first time in the year in question.

For a number of the 64 cells, the result was no institution and, therefore, the volume of students enrolled was also zero. For a number of other cells, government statistics are published and were used. This is especially the case for government distance training institutions and for open universities. In certain countries, the volume of students enrolled in proprietary institutions at a distance must also be declared by regulation.

Once these statistics were collated, the Delphi group of experts gave their statistics for the remaining cells. Again, these statistics were put through three iterations.

A final element of the study to establish the market volume, was to evaluate for each of the 64 cells, the average price paid per enrolment by the student enrolling (or by other taxpayers for the student enrolling) and eventually this was averaged out over the 64 cells at a figure of just under €400 per person per year.

For all the 64 cells, a range of programmes that looked like distance training was excluded from the calculation of statistics and from the calculation of fees paid. These were children's education at a distance, in-house distance training, non-traditional training programmes that did not meet the criteria of the definition, hobby courses, teach-yourself books, technology-based training and computer-based training packages, multimedia packages and courses that formed part of projects, plans, hopes or ideas for the future.

Dangers

There are dangers in doing a census study and publishing its results. The fundamental one is that everybody knows more about a census than the researcher. Thus, if a government makes a census of the population, no matter how meticulous its instruments may be, it is the individual household, and not the government researchers, which knows whether the figure returned to the statistics collectors should be five or seven rather than the six entered into the statistical data bank.

In a similar way, in this study, it is felt that for each of the 64 cells, except for those which are ranked zero, there may be a person or persons who have more accurate data on that particular cell than the researcher. It is, nevertheless, felt that the overall pattern is valid and statistical accuracy for distance training provision, as defined, of plus or minus five per cent is claimed for all of the 64 cells, except for the four UK cells, where the use of varying terminology renders such precision impossible.

12 National profiles

Data collection

The aim of this chapter is to give reliable data on the provision of distance training, as defined, in the EU for planners, analysts and policy-makers, as well as for the general reader. The context is that of demonstrating the national solutions chosen for addressing the challenges of structuring systems for people studying at a distance. Only courses that are available to the public are considered.

Taking stock of a sector of educational provision requires accurate data. Therefore it was decided to count all instances of provision as a basis for this book. As stated in Chapter 11, it was considered impossible and unnecessary to count every person studying at a distance in the whole world.

Instead, it was decided to count every institutional provider, and every enrolment in every institutional provider, and every fee paid for every enrolment in every institutional provider, in every country in the EU at the turn of the millennium.

It was considered that this would give an adequate factual basis for stocktaking and that the patterns identified would be, more or less, repeated throughout the world.

It was not considered that other educational research methodologies or statistical projections would be capable of providing the data required. Only a census study, undertaken as explained in the previous chapter, can provide this data.

With Belgium being counted twice, the EU was divided into 64 cells and data collected on each. The data are presented here under these headings:

1   National characteristics as a context for distance training:

   - Constitution
   - Size and population at 1.1.2000
   - Workforce at 1.1.2000
   - Per capita GDP (Gross Domestic Product) at PPP (Purchasing Power Parities) ranking at 1.1.2000

2   Distance education and training
3   Government distance training institutions

4   Proprietary distance training institutions
5   Open universities
6   Distance training courses from universities
7   Statistics.

It is to be remembered that this is a factual, non-judgemental, analysis of provision. Government training provision may focus on face-to-face provision in training centres or colleges to the exclusion of distance training, and no comment is offered on this. Again, a government may decide whether or not to create an open university, or a government distance training institution, in accordance with national training policies. Keegan and Rumble (1982) provided planning guidelines for states or nations when deciding on national distance training universities or colleges, and these are repeated here because they are believed to be still valid:

- The costs associated with the establishment of an infrastructure for a distance teaching institution and the preparation of sufficient course materials to support a degree programme are high, and require a guaranteed annual volume of student enrolments if the system is to be cost-efficient.
- If sufficient numbers of students cannot be guaranteed, provision of distance training from an existing department of an institute is preferable.
- The number of students at which an autonomous distance training institution becomes more efficient than a mixed-mode institution depends on the choice of media, the extent of student support services, and the number of courses on offer, as well as the costs of conventional education in the country concerned. It lies in the range of 9,000 to 22,000 enrolments a year. (Keegan and Rumble 1982:245–6)

This means that the smaller countries in the EU would not consider founding an open university or college.

In the national profiles, parity of esteem is given to further education and to higher education provision, and also to public and private provision. Statistics are calculated on the basis of the volume of citizens who chose to enrol themselves in a distance training programme in the year in question, or for whom a distance training programme was provided from taxpayers' money.

Austria

1   National characteristics

Austria is a federal republic consisting of nine provinces. Austria is about 580km long and has an area of 83,845sq km. Population 7,883,000. GDP per head at current market prices and PPP in 2000: 113 (4th). EUR15 = 100. The workforce is divided as follows: 8.3 per cent agriculture, 31.1 per cent industry, and 60.6 per cent services.

2   Distance education and training

There is no open university in Austria, nor, at the turn of the millennium, were there any distance education courses for degree credit originating from and developed by Austrian universities. A plan to develop a government distance training institution in the mid-1990s does not yet seem to be completed. The main private providers are grouped in the ÖFV (Austrian Distance Training Association).

3   Government distance training institutions

In the mid-1990s an initiative by the federal government and the government of the city of Vienna, called the *Österreichischer Zentrum für Selbstudium und Fernunterricht* (Austrian Centre for Self-study and Distance Training) was planned, on the government distance training institute model, but does not yet appear to be enrolling students. There is a well-established Austrian Federal Military Distance Training Institute, and some provision from semi-state bodies.

4   Proprietary distance training institutions

The *Österreichischen Fernschulverband* (Austrian Distance Training Association) was founded in 1970 for the development of government and proprietary distance training in Austria. Its list of members has a total of 8,000 enrolments per year for courses which fall within the distance training definition adopted in this study. A further 15,000 enrolments per year are registered with colleges outside their association.

5   Open universities

None.

6   Distance training courses from universities

There is no university programme developed at a distance and offered by an Austrian university. Austrian students therefore enrol at the German Fernuniversität or the British Open University and there are collaborative distance study centres in Vienna, Bregenz and Linz. There is a growing interest in offering courses on the WWW but, as yet, few full degree programmes for adults who do not attend a university.

7   Statistics

Government distance training institutions	9,900
Proprietary distance training institutions	26,000
Open universities	0
Distance training courses from conventional universities	1,000
Total	*36,900*

Belgium

1 National characteristics

The kingdom of Belgium is a parliamentary democracy and a hereditary monarchy. Belgium is a federal state consisting of regions and communities. Legislative power at federal level is exercised jointly by the King, the Chamber of Representatives and the Senate. The three regions are Brussels, Flanders and Wallonia. The three communities are Flemish-, French- and German-speaking Belgians, each with a legislative assembly and an executive. Since 1989, all educational matters have been transferred to the jurisdiction of the communities and the regions, and the Flemish, French and German councils have legislative power over education and training.

Belgium is about 282km long and about 145km wide and has an area of 30,528sq km. Population 10,100,631. GDP per head at current market prices and PPP in 2000: 113 (4th). The workforce is divided as follows: 3 per cent in agriculture, 29 per cent industry, and 68 per cent in services.

The Flemish-speaking community in Belgium

2 Distance education and training

Flanders has a major distance training college run by its government called Bestuur Afstandsonderwijs (Distance Education Service).

A once-flourishing proprietary distance education service is now almost non-existant. An attempt at university-level distance education provision from a consortium, known as the StOHO, was closed by the government of Flanders in March 1997.

3 Government distance training institutions

The Distance Training College of the government Ministry of the Flemish Community of Belgium is located in the centre of Brussels. It is administered by the permanent education section of the Department of Education, was founded in 1959, and formed part of a joint French/Flemish provision until 1968. It enrols 25,000 adults per year in a range of 70 courses and is free. It has at least 50,000 students enrolled at any one time.

4 Proprietary distance training institutions

The commercial distance training sector is represented today by one Flanders-based institution in Brussels, with an annual enrolment of several hundred. There is a rapidly developing range of private initiatives from major Belgian corporations, but these are mainly for in-house staff training.

5   Open universities

None.

6   Distance training courses from universities

The closure of the StOHO by the government of Flanders in March 1997 left distance education at university level in Flanders without a focus and represented a government decision to replace funding for university-level distance education with the funding of technological innovation in conventional education. More conventional universities are providing courses, or parts of courses, on the World Wide Web.

7   Statistics

Government distance training institutions	25,500
Proprietary distance training institutions	300
Open universities	0
Distance training courses from conventional universities	900
Total	26,700

The French-speaking community in Belgium

2   Distance education and training

Wallonia has a major distance training college run by its government and called Enseignment à Distance de la Communauté Française de Belgique. There may still be some provision from government employment agencies and from survivors of a once-flourishing proprietary sector. At university level there is a growing interest in distance provision from Belgian universities, both by 'traditional' distance education courses, and electronically on the World Wide Web.

3   Government distance training institutions

The Service de l'Enseignement à Distance de la Communauté Française de Belgique was founded in 1959. Today it offers 150 courses to about 50,000 students of whom 13,500 are newly enrolled each year. This provision was free up until 1993 when a small administrative charge was introduced.

4   Proprietary distance training institutions

There are a few private distance education colleges, the remnant of a once-flourishing sector 20 years ago.

5 *Open universities*

None.

6 *Distance training courses from universities*

The University of Liège has been at the forefront of research and development in distance education courses and is today being joined by a range of universities in Wallonia which are beginning to make their courses available on the World Wide Web.

7 *Statistics*

Government distance training institutions	13,000
Proprietary distance training institutions	2,500
Open universities	0
Distance training courses from conventional universities	950
Total	*16,450*

Denmark

1 *National characteristics*

The kingdom of Denmark is a constitutional monarchy and parliamentary democracy. Denmark comprises more than 400 islands in the Baltic and North seas together with the Jutland peninsula and measures about 338km from north to south. The population is 5,180,614. GDP per head at current market prices at PPP in 2000: 114 (3rd). The workforce is divided as follows: 6 per cent agriculture, 26 per cent industry and 68 per cent services.

2 *Distance education and training*

The country is small, has good educational facilities, is rich in technology and has educational institutions at less than an hour's distance from most citizens. Danish educational policy tends to focus on group-based institutions and travel to a centre, but electronic provision at university level is growing rapidly.

3 *Government distance training institutions*

The Military Academy is an important user of distance education for civil as well as military courses. There is, in addition, a series of courses from a number of technical colleges.

4   Proprietary distance training institutions

A series of take-overs has led to the creation of one major proprietary provider, which provides maritime courses at further education level, and is starting to offer higher education on the World Wide Web.

5   Open universities

There is no open university but Åarhus University uses the name 'Jutland Open University' for its distance education programme.

6   Distance training courses from universities

At Danish universities there is a continuum of provision from full face-to-face to night classes with distance education considered a method of delivery and not a field of educational endeavour. Apart from the Jutland Open University and the Copenhagen Business School, a number of other universities have distance education courses and are developing courses on the internet.

7   Statistics

Government distance training institutions	18,000
Proprietary distance training institutions	3,400
Open universities	0
Distance training courses from conventional universities	2,000
Total	*23,400*

Finland

1   National characteristics

Finland is a sovereign republican state. Nearly one-third of the country lies north of the Arctic Circle and the country has a total area of 338,145sq km of which over 33,000sq km is inland water. The population is 5,054,982. GDP per head at current market prices and PPP in 2000 is 102 (9th). The workforce is divided as follows: 6 per cent agriculture, 21 per cent industry and 73 per cent services.

2   Distance education and training

Finland's history of distance education goes back 80 years and there is extensive provision today. It has 21 universities, all of which are technology-rich and all have distance education programmes. Almost all of the 600 vocational colleges in Finland offer some kind of multiple-form training, which may include distance education. In the terminology used in this study, there is no open university; rather what is referred to as 'the open university' in Finland is a study system based on co-operation among universities. The universities have a rich and highly developed presence on the internet and provide courses on the World Wide Web.

3 Government distance training institutions

Public provision of distance training courses is organised from vocational colleges and is estimated at 20,000 enrolments per year. The government has given these colleges responsibility for the unemployed, in collaboration with the continuing education departments of conventional universities. There is also extensive provision from the Finnish military academy.

4 Proprietary distance training institutions

Private provision is in decline despite an impressive tradition going back nearly 80 years. Today the focus of Finnish education is on information technology from technology-rich universities and the concept of correspondence is not in fashion. There is, however, a range of marketing institutions which have adapted their traditional distance education provision to the new technology and which continue to prosper.

5 Open universities

In the terminology adopted by this report there is no open university. There was an extensive debate in Finland in the 1980s, about whether a country, with a dispersed population, with advanced communications technology, and with a long history of teaching at a distance should found an open university. The final decision favoured individual programmes from the conventional universities. Today all 21 of these universities are centres of communications technology and all run distance education or open learning projects. All these universities have programmes in further education and in continuing education and have been given the task of providing courses for the unemployed.

6 Distance training courses from universities

The Finnish Association for Distance Education, FADE, is an association for universities and organisations which offer higher education at a distance. The International Association for Continuing Education is another important provider, based at the centre for continuing education at the Helsinki University of Technology. All the Finnish universities, with the exception of the very smallest, arrange open university teaching. The Universities of Helsinki, Turku, Tampere and Jyväskylä are leading providers.

The Virtual Open University is a nationwide project, under the Ministry of Education's 1997–2000 information strategy programme and provides studies leading to a form of academic achievement via the World Wide Web.

7 *Statistics*

Government distance training institutions	20,000
Proprietary distance training institutions	14,000
Open universities	0
Distance training courses from conventional universities	47,500
Total	*81,500*

France

1 *National characteristics*

France is a republic in which power is shared between the president, the government and the National Assembly. There are four overseas departments, four overseas territories and two territorial collectives. The total area of metropolitan France is 543,965sq km. The population is 58,000,000. The GDP per head at current market prices and PPP in the year 2000 is 103 (8th). The workforce is divided as follows: 6 per cent agriculture, 30 per cent industry and 64 per cent services.

2 *Distance education and training*

The government of France founded a major distance training institution, the CNED, in 1939. There are, in addition, other major government-funded and para-public distance training providers in France. There is no open university but 20 conventional universities have departments of distance education. The private sector appears to be in decline.

3 *Government distance training institutions*

Government distance training institutions in France can be divided into public and para-public. The public ones include the CNED, AFPA, CNAM and CNPR. There is an additional range of para-public distance training providers. The CNED, with over 405,000 students in the year 2000, is Europe's largest distance educational provision via a government, with 200,000 of its students at university level. AFPA and CNPR and INTEC are other major providers from a rich government distance training sector.

4 *Proprietary distance training institutions*

The provision of distance education from proprietary institutions in France is divided into those who are members of the industry association CHANED and those that are not members. In many of these institutions, enrolments in the year 2000 seem to be in decline.

5 Open universities

None.

6 Distance training courses from universities

Distance training courses from universities are best analysed as (i) members of the FIED (Fédération Interuniversitaire de l'Enseignement à Distance), (ii) the IUTs (University Technological Institutes) and (iii) other universities, which are not members of FIED, and a wide range of France's 86 universities which plan to or already offer courses on the World Wide Web.

7 Statistics

Government distance training institutions	440,000
Proprietary distance training institutions	45,000
Open universities	0
Distance training courses from conventional universities	47,000
Total	*532,000*

Germany

1 National characteristics

The Federal Republic of Germany is a parliamentary democracy with a federal constitution and is comprised of 16 states (*Länder*) which have exclusive responsibility for education. Germany has an area of 248,577sq km and a population of 80,974,632. The GDP per head at current market prices and PPP in the year 2000 is 106 (6th). The workforce is divided as follows: 3 per cent agriculture, 39 per cent industry and 58 per cent services.

2 Distance education and training

Germany has an open university, the Fernuniversität-Gesamthochschule in Hagen, and a number of distance education initiatives from its conventional universities and technical colleges. There is a large private sector, statistics from which are published annually by government regulation.

3 Government distance training institutions

For the purposes of this study the provision of distance training and of courses on the internet, from a range of colleges of technology (*Fachhochschulen*), is grouped here.

Radio-based provision known as the Funkkolleg and television-based provision known as Telekolleg, seem to be in decline.

4 Proprietary distance training institutions

There are 108 private institutions offering distance education courses in the year 2000, 51 of which are members of the German Distance Training Association (DFV), with an important contribution from AKAD which has three distance polytechnics. The members of the private distance training sector in Germany must have their courses assessed and approved by a government agency before enrolments can be accepted and their statistics are published annually by regulation.

5 Open universities

Planning for a German open university began in the mid-1960s. After extensive discussions, the State of North Rhine-Westphalia founded its own open university, the Fernuniversität, in 1974. Within the structures of this open university there is a virtual university (*Virtuelle Universität*), a World Wide Web-based structure within the open university structure.

6 Distance training courses from universities

A range of conventional Germany universities now teach at a distance and many provide courses on the World Wide Web.

7 Statistics

Government distance training institutions	48,000
Proprietary distance training institutions	150,000
Open universities	61,809
Distance training courses from conventional universities	31,849
Total	*291,658*

Greece

1 National characteristics

Greece is a parliamentary democracy divided into 13 regions. The National Ministry of Education and Religion carries responsibility for the implementation of educational laws, degrees and directives. The total area is 131,957sq km, of which about one-fifth is composed of islands. Population is 10,259,900. GDP per head at current market prices in 2000: 69 (15th). The workforce is divided as follows: 21 per cent agriculture, 28 per cent industry and 51 per cent services.

2 Distance education and training

The government of Greece in 1997 decided to create an open university called *Elliniko Anikto Panepistemio*, the seventh open university in the EU, with a goal of reaching 40,000 student enrolments within a few years of its opening. This is a remarkable development in a country in which previously distance training was little-known and educational technology played only a small role.

3 Government distance training institutions

None.

4 Proprietary distance training institutions

There is one small college.

5 Open universities

The Hellenic Open University is a state public open university. It is based in Patras, with faculties in human studies, social science, applied arts, science and technology. Should the government goal of 40,000 students in the first few years be achieved, this university will bring Greece quickly to the forefront of distance training provision in Europe.

6 Distance training courses from universities

At the time of writing, there appeared to be little distance provision from Greek universities.

7 Statistics

Government distance training institutions	0
Proprietary distance training institutions	60
Open universities	1,000
Distance training courses from conventional universities	0
Total	*1,060*

Ireland

1 National characteristics

Ireland is a parliamentary democracy. The Republic of Ireland is 68,895sq km in area, with a population of 3,525,719, measuring 486km by 280km at its widest points. GDP per head at current market prices and PPP in 2000 is 122 (2nd). The workforce has 14 per cent agriculture, 29 per cent industry and 57 per cent services.

2   Distance education and training

The major provider is the National Distance Education Centre at Dublin City University. The private sector is still the largest in terms of citizens enrolled but the relative gap with the public sector has closed. Many of the new endeavours are in the public institutions in Ireland.

3   Government distance training institutions

None.

4   Proprietary distance training institutions

Ten private or semi-private distance training providers enrol annually an estimated 10,000 students.

5   Open university

None.

6   Distance training courses from universities

The National Distance Centre is a Faculty of Dublin City University and there is a growing provision from other universities and from the Regional Institutes of Technology, with a growth of distance education on the web.

7   Statistics

Government distance training institutions	0
Proprietary distance training institutions	10,300
Open universities	0
Distance training courses from conventional universities	11,900
Total	*22,200*

Italy

1   National characteristics

Italy is a parliamentary republic with an area of 301,277sq km. The population is 57,138,489. GDP per head at current market prices and PPP in 2000: 100 (10th).

The workforce has 9 per cent agriculture, 32 per cent industry and 59 per cent in services.

2 Distance education and training

The major provider is the University of Rome III and there are some courses from other universities and from the Consorzio Nettuno. Attempts to offer distance training from government providers have not been maintained and the private sector is in decline.

3 Government distance training institutions

None.

4 Proprietary distance training institutions

The private sector is represented today by a Turin Institute, which has purchased the remaining private distance education colleges in Italy. An important development is Trainet, developed by the Italian Telecom Group, which started by offering distance education internally for the training of Italian Telecom staff, and some years ago broadened its market to include students from other business groupings as well.

5 Open universities

None.

6 Distance training courses from universities

The major provider is the University of Rome III and there is also a small university provision from the Universities of Florence, Ferrara, the Politechnico di Milano, with a developing interest among the universities in providing web-based courses.

There are a number of consortia, usually groupings of universities and other bodies, of which the best-known is the Consorzio Nettuno, which offers courses by satellite. Another consortium, the Consorzio per l'Università a Distanza (CUD), was closed in the late 1990s.

7 Statistics

Government distance training institutions	0
Proprietary distance training institutions	65,000
Open universities	0
Distance training courses from conventional universities	10,000
Total	*75,000*

Luxembourg

1 National characteristics

Luxembourg is a representative democracy and constitutional monarchy. Executive power lies with the Grand Duke. It is exercised by the members of the government under the co-ordinating authority of the Prime Minister. The country has an area of 2,586sq km and a population of 389,800. Per capita GDP at current market prices and PPP in 2000 is 175 (1st).

2 Distance education and training

There is no official provision of training at a distance from government structures. Nor are there any proprietary distance training structures based in Luxembourg. Connections with educational institutions, usually in Germany, enable distance learning and training courses to be followed.

3 Government distance training institutions

None.

4 Proprietary distance training institutions

None.

5 Open universities

None.

6 Distance training courses from universities

None.

7 Statistics

Government distance training institutions	0
Proprietary distance training institutions	0
Open universities	0
Distance training courses from conventional universities	0
Total	*0*

The Netherlands

1 National characteristics

The Kingdom of the Netherlands is a parliamentary democracy and hereditary monarchy. The Queen and the Cabinet constitute the government, which has a parliament, which consists of the Upper House and the Lower House. The Netherlands has a total area of 41,526sq km and a population of 15,385,000. GDP per head at current market prices and PPP in 2000: 105 (7th). The workforce is divided as follows: 5 per cent agriculture, 26 per cent industry and 69 per cent services.

2 Distance education and training

The Netherlands has an open university, the Open universiteit at Heerlen. There is growth in provision of continuing education courses at a distance from many of its universities and on the World Wide Web. There is a television-based vocational training provider, TELEAC, but there seems to be little or no government distance training provision at the further education level. The private sector is active and competent.

3 Government distance training institutions

Although there is extensive computer-based training and training on the World Wide Web, there seems to be no government further education courses at a distance that would fall within the definition of distance education in this study. For the purposes of this report, the Television Academy (TELEAC) is included here, as the state makes contributions to its transmissions facilities.

4 Proprietary distance education institutions

The private sector is vigorous and competent and a leader in EU proprietary provision. Many of the colleges now provide higher education and university-level programmes and include e-mail for assignment correction and offer a wide range of courses. The move to higher education courses and higher technology courses seems to have given the sector a new lease of life, added to a change in government policy which enables these institutions to collaborate with conventional universities and other providers, for courses for which the government does not choose to provide. Included here is the Charkov Beheer at Nijmegen with over 400,000 enrolments, mainly from Eastern Europe.

5 Open universities

The Dutch Open University was created in 1984 and is located at Heerlen, in the extreme south of the country.

6   Distance training courses from universities

There is a growing range of MBAs, business degrees, internet courses and franchise courses from conventional Dutch universities. These do not teach the Dutch university degree at a distance, as this is the work of the Open Universiteit, but there is rapid growth of provision in continuing education. University of Twente is one of a number of Dutch universities which have made impressive contributions to the development of courses on the World Wide Web.

7   Statistics

Government distance training institutions	50,000
Proprietary distance training institutions	580,000
Open universities	28,000
Distance training courses from conventional universities	10,000
Total	*668,000*

Portugal

1   National characteristics

Portugal is a parliamentary republic with legislative power exercised by parliament, which has one chamber. The total area is 92,082sq km and the population is 9,862,700. The 2000 GDP per head at current market prices is 75 (14th) and the workforce is divided as follows: 18 per cent agriculture, 34 per cent industry and 48 per cent services.

2   Distance education and training

Portugal has a distance teaching university, founded in 1988, and a centre for business executive training at a distance. There is a range of semi-private and private structures which provide distance training.

3   Government distance training institutions

Programmes are provided by the Institute for Quality and Soldering of the Portuguese Business and Training Institute and CET Portugal Telcom.

4   Proprietary distance education institutions

CIT in Lisbon is the largest proprietary distance training provider in Portugal, founded in 1960, but the market is more and more dominated by large Spanish distance training colleges.

5 Open university

The Universidade Aberta was created in 1988 and is an official higher education institution with about 10,000 students.

6 Distance training courses from universities

The DISLOGO programme from the Catholic University of Portugal is a postgraduate distance education programme for executives in business and banking which started in 1994.

7 Statistics

Government distance training institutions	11,000
Proprietary distance training institutions	2,000
Open universities	11,000
Distance training courses from conventional universities	300
Total	*24,300*

Spain

1 National characteristics

Spain is a constitutional hereditary monarchy and parliamentary democracy. Since 1983 there have been 17 autonomous communities in Spain, each with its own parliament and executive. The area of Spain is 504,782sq km and the population is 30,143,394. Per capita GDP in PPP in 2000 is 83 (13th). The workforce is divided as follows: 11 per cent agriculture, 33 per cent industry and 56 per cent services.

2 Distance education and training

Spain is by far the largest provider in Europe of distance training for vocational qualifications. This is little recognised in the literature and little realised by government and educational planners who often consider distance education to be a North European and North American priority. Spain has two open universities, a government distance training institution, and a large proprietary sector, enrolling over 400,000 students per year.

3 Government distance training institutions

The CIDEAD, the government distance training provider, was established in 1992, from previous foundations dating back to 1975. Today it has 15,000 students in vocational studies at a distance, 30,000 in adult second-chance education, and 60,000 in English courses at a distance.

4   Proprietary distance education institutions

Over 400,000 students per year enrol in distance training courses from the proprietary sector in Spain. The main colleges are represented by a national organisation called the *Asociación Nacional de Centros de Enseñanza a Distancia* (ANCED), which regulates its members' qualifications and publicity. The strength of the proprietary sector in Spain is attributed to a new apprenticeship contract, the support of distance courses by the state, by the EU and by large companies, and the prestige and the reputation of ANCED and its members. Radio ECCA, part public and part non-profit making, enrols 90,000 per year in its radio-based distance courses in the Canary Islands and mainland Spain (Palmés 1999).

5   Open universities

Spain has two open universities: the Universidad Nacional de Educación a Distancia (UNED) in Madrid and the Universitat Oberta de Catalunya (UOC) in Barcelona. Planning for an open university in Spain began in the mid-1960s and was successfully completed by 1970. The university's charter was granted in August 1972 and the first students enrolled in 1973. With over 170,000 students enrolled in the year 2000, UNED is Europe's largest open university, with the same status as conventional universities in Spain and with students able to transfer credit between UNED and the other universities.

The autonomous region of Catalonia founded a distance training university in 1995. Because it is the creation of the autonomous community, it has a particular focus on the Catalán language and culture. The UOC has based its didactic structure on the construction of a virtual campus and describes itself as a virtual rather than an open university, seeking to link its students electronically throughout Barcelona and the rest of Catalonia.

6   Distance training courses from universities

The Spanish government, with two open universities, does not encourage its conventional universities to enrol students who choose not to study at their campuses.

7   Statistics

Government distance training institutions	110,000
Proprietary distance training institutions	420,000
Open universities	190,000
Distance training courses from conventional universities	400
Total	*720,400*

Sweden

1 National characteristics

Sweden is a constitutional monarchy with a parliamentary form of government. The King has ceremonial functions as head of state. Sweden has a total area of 449,964sq km with a population of 8,745,109. Sweden has per capita GDP in 2000 of 96 compared with the EUR 15 average of 100 and ranks 12th in the EU. Its workforce is divided as follows: 3 per cent agriculture, 29 per cent industry and 68 per cent services.

2 Distance education and training

On the secondary and upper secondary levels two national institutes for distance education were founded, one in the northern part of Sweden and one in the south.

At the tertiary level Sweden chose not to build a centralised distance university but instead an extremely decentralised system was created. The responsibility for carrying out distance education rested with individual university departments, which at the same time organised traditional forms of university education.

The national broadcasting company has a special assignment to arrange distance education courses for popular education.

3 Government distance training institutions

Distance training from public or semi-public bodies is offered by a range of *Hogskolan* which provide courses which usually involve periods of intensive study at the college, alternating with periods of study at home. The armed forces have developed courses for personnel training by means of distance study methods.

4 Proprietary distance training institutions

A once-flourishing proprietary distance education sector has largely been dispersed, with government policy promoting enrolment in state-supported colleges, in programmes which combine some distance study with face-to-face periods at college, and the introduction of a wide range of open and flexible courses, which makes the identification of distance programmes difficult.

5 Open universities

None.

6 Distance training courses from conventional universities

Sweden has a series of either open programmes or distance education programmes from its conventional universities. The major providers are part of the Swedish

Consortium for Distance Education (SCDE), which includes the Universities of Lund, Linköping, Umeå, Uppsala, the Royal Institute of Technology and the University College of Växjö.

7 Statistics

Government distance training institutions	15,000
Proprietary distance training institutions	9,000
Open universities	0
Distance training courses from conventional universities	35,000
Total	*59,000*

United Kingdom

1 National characteristics

The UK is a constitutional, hereditary monarchy. Executive power is entrusted by the sovereign to the leader of the majority party in the House of Commons, who then becomes Prime Minister. Area is 242,752sq km; population 58,000,000. GDP per head at current market prices in 2000: 98 (11th). The workforce is divided as follows: 2 per cent agriculture, 28 per cent industry and 70 per cent services.

2 Distance education and training

At university level the model reflects the same strong voluntarist tradition that characterises face-to-face provision: an open university and at least 100 conventional universities competing for the distance education market.

At further education level there is a range of further education colleges offering either open or flexible or distance training programmes in competition with a still strong private sector of 45 registered providers and an uncountable number of, usually small, private providers of distance training programmes. A UK government agency has recently issued its quality control in distance learning document to maintain quality of provision at a distance.

3 Government distance training institutions

The Further Education Funding Council is the government body that oversees the further education and training colleges in Britain. Today the UK has a range of open learning and distance training providers of the types described. The distinction between open learning and distance training is hard to establish. In the further education area, open learning is dominant. Basically this means that a wide range of providers are in competition with each other for survival and for the market. The basic model is that of corporate management training providers who provide resource-based in-company training with freelance tutors who work in the company for in-depth sessions on an occasional basis.

4 Proprietary distance training institutions

The Open and Distance Learning Quality Council (ODLQC) groups a range of proprietary distance training institutions and has links to other sectors. Enrolments at the institutions that are members are said to be about 100,000 per year, with an additional 10 to 20 per cent from a range of, usually, smaller colleges that are not affiliated.

5 Open universities

The OUUK at Milton Keynes was created by Royal Charter in 1969 and enrolled its first students in 1971. It has 13 regional offices and 306 study centres in the UK and 46 overseas. It has made extensive developments in the countries of Central and Eastern Europe and in 1999 opened another open university in the US called the Open University of the United States. Its ranking in academic excellence is discussed in Chapter 7.

6 Distance training courses from universities

The UK university-level model is to have over 100 conventional universities competing for the distance university market with the Open University. These university-level distance providers include: the external degree programme of the University of London, providers of MBAs and other business degrees at a distance, the Open Learning Foundation – a grouping of former polytechnic universities which teach at a distance, a wide range of universities which are offering courses or parts of courses on the WWW.

7 Statistics

Government distance training institutions	128,000
Proprietary distance training institutions	124,000
Open universities	165,000
Distance training courses from conventional universities	84,000
Total	*501,000*

Country	Government provision	Proprietary provision	Open university	Other universities	Totals
Austria	9,900	26,000	0	1,000	36,900
Belgium FL	25,500	300	0	900	26,700
Belgium FR	13,000	2,500	0	950	16,450
Denmark	18,000	3,400	0	2,000	23,400
Finland	20,000	14,000	0	47,500	81,500
France	440,000	45,000	0	47,000	532,000
Germany	48,000	150,000	61,809	31,849	291,658
Greece	0	60	1,000	0	1,060
Ireland	0	10,300	0	11,900	22,200
Italy	0	65,000	0	10,000	75,000
Luxembourg	0	0	0	0	0
Netherlands	50,000	580,000	28,000	10,000	668,000
Portugal	11,000	2,000	11,000	300	24,300
Spain	110,000	420,000	190,000	400	720,400
Sweden	15,000	9,000	0	35,000	59,000
United Kingdom	128,000	124,000	165,000	84,000	501,000
Totals	**888,400**	**1,451,560**	**456,809**	**282,799**	**3,079,568**

Figure 12.1 Distance training statistics: EU 1999

References

Amundsen, C. and Collinge, J. (1999) 'Educational Technology and Distance Education', in G. Weidenfeld and D. Keegan (eds) *L'Enseignement à distance à l'aube du troisième millénaire*. Poitiers: CNED.

Bååth, J. (1980) *Postal Two-way Communication in Correspondence Education*. Lund: Gleerup.

Bates, A. (1995) *Technology, Open Learning and Distance Education*. London: Routledge.

Boshier, R. *et al.* (1997) 'Best and Worst Dressed Web Courses: Strutting into the Twenty-first Century in Comfort and Style', *Distance Education* 18, 2, 327–49.

—— *et al.* (1998) 'World Wide America? Think Globally, Click Locally', *Distance Education* 19, 1, 109–23.

Boyd, W. and King, E. (1969) *The History of Western Education*. London: Black.

Bramble, W. (1996) 'The Florida Teletraining Project: Military Training with Two-way Compressed Video', *The American Journal of Distance Education*, 9, 1, 6–26.

Cairncross, F. (1997) *The Death of Distance*. London: Orion.

Clark, R. (1983) 'Reconsidering Research on Learning from Media', *Review of Educational Research*, 53, 4, 445–59.

Collis, B. (1996) *Telelearning in a Digital World: The Future of Distance Learning*. London: Thompson.

Collis, B. and Peters, O. (1999) 'At the Frontier: Asynchronous Video and the WWW for New Forms of Learning', in G. Weidenfeld and D. Keegan (eds) *L'Enseignement à distance à l'aube du troisième millénaire*. Poitiers: CNED.

Coombs, P. (1985) *The World Crisis in Education*. London: OUP.

Corrigan, D. (1998) *CASO's Internet University. Your Guide to Online College Courses*. Harwich, MA: Cape Software.

Dalkey, N. (1969) 'An Experimental Study of Group Opinion', *Futures*, 1, 5, 408–26.

Daniel, Sir J. (1996) *Mega-universities and Knowledge Media: Technology Strategies for Higher Education*. London: Kogan Page.

—— (1999) Speeches of the Vice-Chancellor of the Open University, http://www.open.ac.uk/OU/News/VC.html (1.12.1999).

Dubin, R. and Taveggia, T. (1968) *The Teaching-Learning Paradox. A Comparative Analysis of College Teaching Methods*. Eugene: University of Oregon.

Duning, B. (1993) 'The Coming of the New Distance Educators in the United States: The Telecommunications Generation Takes off', in K. Harry, M. John and D. Keegan (eds) *Distance Education: New Perspectives*. London: Routledge.

Fritsch, H. (1997) *Host Contacted, Waiting for Reply*. Hagen: ZIFF

—— (1998) *Document Done*. Hagen: ZIFF.

Garrison, D. (1985) 'Three Generations of Technological Innovation in Distance Education', *Distance Education*, 6, 32, 235–41.

Garrison, D. and Shale, D. (eds) (1987) *Education at a Distance: From Issues to Practice*. Malabar: Krieger.

Godfrey, D. *et al*. (1979) *Gutenberg Two. The New Electronics and Social Change*. Toronto: Porcepic.

Hawkridge, D. (1976) 'Next Year Jerusalem. The Rise of Educational Technology', *British Journal of Educational Technology*, 6–30.

Kaye, A. and Rumble, G. (eds) (1981) *Distance Teaching for Higher and Adult Education*. London: Croom Helm.

Keegan, D. (1993) *Very Large Distance Education Systems: The Case of China*. Hagen: ZIFF.

—— (1995a) 'Teaching and Learning by Satellite in a European Virtual Classroom', in F. Lockwood (ed.) *Open and Distance Learning Today*. London: Routledge, 108–18.

—— (1995b) *Distance Education Technology for the New Millennium: Compressed Video Teaching*. Hagen: ZIFF.

—— (1996) *Foundations of Distance Education* (3rd edn). London: Routledge.

Keegan, D. and Rumble, G. (1982) 'Characteristics of the Distance Teaching Universities', in G. Rumble and K. Harry (eds) *The Distance Teaching Universities*. London: Croom Helm.

Kozma, R. (1991) 'Learning with Media', *Review of Educational Research*, 61, 2, 179–211.

Mason, R. (1998) *Globalising Education: Trends and Applications*. London: Routledge.

McGreal, R. (1999) 'TeleEducation Database of Online Courses', http://cuda.teleeducation.nb.ca/ (1.12.1999).

McVey, G. (1970) 'Television: Some Viewer Display Considerations', *AV Communication Review*, 18, 3, 277–90.

Miller, E. and Rice, A. (1967) *Systems of Organisation. The Control of Task and Sentient Boundaries*. London: Tavistock.

Palmés, C. (1999) 'Radio ECCA. La Radio Educativa', *Revista de Educación y Formación a Distancia*, 23, 29–39.

Paulsen, M.-F. (1999) Courses on the World Wide Web, http://www.nettskolen.com/kurs/ 0000-spice.homeside.html (1/12/1999).

Peters, G. and Daniel, J. (1994) 'Comparison of Public Funding of Distance Education and Other Modes of Higher Education in England', in G. Dhanaragan *et al*. (eds) *Economics of Distance Education: Recent Experience*. Hong Kong: OLI, 31–41.

Peters, O. (1994) *The Industrialization of Teaching and Learning: Otto Peters on Distance Education*. London: Routledge,

Popper, K. (1964) *The Open Society and Its Enemies*. London: Oxford, OUP.

Rekkedal, T. (1984) 'The Written Assignments in Correspondence Education. Effects of Reducing Turn-around time. An Experimental Study', *Distance Education*, 4, 231–50.

Rumble, G. (1997) *The Costs and Economics of Open and Distance Learning*. London: Kogan Page.

Russell, T. (1999) 'The No Significant Difference Phenomenon', http://cuda.teleeducation.nb.ca/nosignificantdifference/(1.12.1999).

Schneiderman, B. (1992) *Designing the User Interface: Strategies for Effective Human–Computer Interaction*. Reading, MA: Addison-Wesley.

Schramm, W. (1977) *Big Media, Little Media*. London: Sage.

Schreiber, D. and Berge, Z. (1998) *Distance Training. How Innovative Organisations Are Using Technology to Maximise Learning and Meet Business Objectives*. San Francisco, CA: Jossey Bass.

Schutte, J.G. (1999) Virtual Teaching in Higher Education: The New Intellectual Superhighway or Just Another Traffic Jam? http://www.csun.edu/sociology/virexp.htm (1.12.1999).

Smith, K. (1979) *External Studies at the University of New England: A Silver Jubilee Review 1954–1979*. Armidale, NSW: UNE.

Van den Brande, L. (1993) *Flexible and Distance Learning*. Chichester: Wiley.

Van der Mark, D. (1993) *Directory of Private Distance Education Institutes and Associations in Europe*. Arnhem: AECS.

Wei, R. (1997) *China's Radio and TV Universities and the British Open University: A Comparative Perspective*. Hagen: ZIFF.

Winn, W. (1990) 'Media and Instructional Methods', in R. Garrison and D. Shale (eds) *Education at a Distance*. Malabar: Krieger.

World Bank (1999) Glossary of Distance Education, http://www-wbweb4.worldbank.org/disted/glossary.html (1.12.1999).

Index